NOT ABOVE

HEATHER BIRD

NOT ABOVE THE LAW

THE TRAGIC STORY OF
JOANN WILSON
AND
COLIN THATCHER

KEY PORTER BOOKS

Canadian Cataloguing in Publication Data

Bird, Heather, 1958–
  Not above the law

ISBN 0-919493-55-6

1. Thatcher, JoAnn. 2. Thatcher, Colin.
3. Murder — Canada.   4. Trials (Murder) — Canada.
5. Crime and criminals — Canada — Biography.
I. Title.

HV6535.C2B57 1985   364.1'523'0924   C85-098104-2

Key Porter Books Limited
70 The Esplanade
Toronto, Ontario
Canada M5E 1R2

PHOTOGRAPH CREDITS   Canapress: 149, 152;
Canapress/*Times Herald*: 65, 67; Canapress/*Leader Post*: 63 bottom, 68; Canapress/*Star Phoenix*: 154, 155, 156 bottom, 157, 158; Canapress/*Toronto Star*: 150; *Star Phoenix*: cover, 63 top, 64, 66, 69, 70, 151, 153, 156 top.

Cover Design: Brant Cowie/Artplus
Typesetting: Compeer Typographic Services Limited
Printing and Binding: Gagne Printing Limited
Printed and bound in Canada

85 86 87   6 5 4 3 2 1

CONTENTS

CHAPTER ONE

The Murder

At that dusky time of the evening when it is more dark than light, Craig Dotson left his office at the Legislative Building on Albert Street in Regina, Saskatchewan.

It was January 21, 1983, in the depth of a typical Saskatchewan winter. There was so much snow on the sidewalks that Dotson was forced to walk along the middle of the road.

Dotson had worked late that Friday night. As the director of research for the Official Opposition caucus he had had to stay late to make copies of a speech that was to be delivered the following day. Shortly before 6 p.m., he left his office and bundled up in his winter clothes for the trudge home through the snow. He lived about four blocks west of the Legislature, just a few minutes' walk along 20th Avenue, which ran directly west from the building on Albert Street.

Dotson walked out the front doors, down the stairs and across Albert, one of the busiest streets in Regina. Once safely across, the first house he approached on his right-hand side was 2876 Albert, the home of Tony and JoAnn Wilson. The thirty-nine-year-old civil servant didn't know the Wilsons personally, but he knew who they were and where they lived.

Like many of the dwellings in this neighbourhood, the Wilson house was large, a white house with brown trim. The house faced east, directly towards the front steps of the Legislative Building. A corner house, its detached, two-car garage faced south onto 20th Avenue; from it a communicating door led into the house. Electronic surveillance cameras were visible on the property, but they were phonies, simply there for show.

As Dotson, now walking west on 20th Avenue, approached the garage of the Wilson home, a dark green four-door Audi sedan, Saskatchewan licence number KWP 174, overtook him and turned into the right-hand side of the garage.

The driver was JoAnn Wilson, returning home a little later than her usual 5 p.m. from her job at Radius 2 Interiors, an interior design business on Broad Street owned by JoAnn and her husband.

Inside the Wilson home, Maria Lahtinen, the twenty-two-year-old housekeeper, was preparing dinner. Downstairs in the basement, Stephanie Thatcher, JoAnn's daughter from her first marriage — to politician Colin Thatcher — was watching television. Stephanie — a blonde, pert little girl — had celebrated her ninth birthday exactly two weeks earlier. Upstairs in the master bedroom Tony Wilson was in bed with flu. A slim, athletic-looking man with glasses and curly salt-and-pepper hair, Wilson makes a comfortable living as the vice-president of IPSCO, the Interprovincial Pipe and Steel Company Ltd.

Outside in the snow, Dotson paid no particular attention to the Wilson car and continued on his way. He was intent on getting home as soon as possible.

Inside the garage, JoAnn slid from the driver's seat, clutching her purse and her car keys. A slim and attractive brown-eyed blonde, at forty-three she was the mother of three children, all fathered by Colin Thatcher.

JoAnn's eyes had some trouble adjusting to the darkness of the garage. For some reason, the garage lights weren't working that night. To this day, no one knows why.

8

She turned to walk between her Audi and the family station wagon, an Oldsmobile with wood panelling on its sides, which was parked on the left-hand side of the garage. It was then that her killer stepped towards her in the garage. The streetlights shone in through the open garage door and illuminated his face. He held something in his right hand.

JoAnn knew it was the end — the end of the months of terror and anguish she had suffered during her messy divorce from Colin. We do not know — we may never know — whether it was Colin Thatcher himself in the garage that night. The man stepped forward towards JoAnn. The actual murder weapons have never been found, but it's believed the killer held an object similar to a meat cleaver in his hand. The man grabbed her by the collar of her fur coat, wrenching it so tightly it bruised her neck. He held her by the throat with his left hand and began to rain blows down her head with the instrument in his right hand.

JoAnn started to scream with shrill, high-pitched cries like those of a small child. Her purse and her keys clattered to the garage floor as she threw both her hands up to protect herself.

The cleaver descended on her head at least twenty times while she desperately struggled to get away. The instrument was heavy enough and sharp enough to make gashes in her scalp and penetrate to the bone. Some of the blows landed directly on her head; others — partially deflected — only bruised or scraped her skin. JoAnn took at least seven blows to her arms and hands as she tried in vain to save her life. She thrust her head down to protect her face and was repeatedly struck on the top of the head.

The force of the blows was enough to fracture the bone in her left forearm and nearly sever the little finger on her left hand. The bones in the palm of her right hand connected to her little finger and her ring finger were also fractured. There were cuts and bruises all over her head and her hands.

During the attack JoAnn continued to scream. And her cries were heard—by Craig Dotson, hurrying home through the snowy streets.

Dotson had gone a fair distance in the minute or so that had elapsed since he saw JoAnn pull into her garage. He started to hear her cries at about Angus Street, one block west of Albert.

Dotson did not at first pay much attention to the cries. "I thought that they were screams of a child, and I thought that it was a child in some distress of some sort — hung up on a fence was the thing that was in my mind," he explained later.

At first, then, he merely continued on his way, confident that the child's troubles were easily fixed and expecting the crying to stop momentarily. But when the screams persisted, Dotson, despite his lateness, turned back. He retraced his steps down the middle of the road, across Angus Street towards the Wilson house, looking from one side of the street to the other, trying to spot the source of the cries.

Help was on its way; but time was running out for JoAnn inside the garage. Blood was spattered along both sides of the cars in the garage. There were smears all along the panelling of the station wagon, indicating that she swayed against it several times during the beating.

She was alive when her assailant finally stopped beating her. The man forced her to her knees, which later showed bruises from the hard garage floor. He dragged her about twelve feet on her knees and then pulled out what was probably a .357 magnum revolver.

Dotson was approaching the house by this time, still walking at his normal pace. He was within seconds of finding what he was looking for.

Maybe JoAnn's killer told her what he intended to

do. She let out one final, bloodcurdling scream, louder, shriller and more high-pitched than all the rest. Dotson heard a crack, a sudden loud noise, then silence.

JoAnn was shot just above the root of the right ear. The hollow-point, aluminum-coated, silver-tipped bullet exploded into numerous fragments as it entered her brain. Her face smacked into the garage floor as her body slumped forward. That fall accounted for the scrapes and bruises that the pathologist later found on her face.

Her killer calmly walked out of the garage and stopped for a second. Craig Dotson was standing in the middle of the street, directly in front of the lane that ran behind the garage. The killer was wearing dark clothing — dark pants and a dark three-quarter-length jacket. He had a shaggy or scraggly beard and dark hair. His right hand was hidden under his coat as if concealing something, Dotson couldn't see what; he caught only a fleeting glimpse of the man in the dusk.

Dotson continued along the middle of the street a few paces, looking right and left, then, on his left, spotted a body lying face down. Realizing then that the dark-clad man must have some connection to the body, he ran back to the alley and looked north along it. But by then the killer was nowhere in sight.

Dotson became very frightened. He knew something was wrong, drastically wrong, and he didn't know if the killer would return for him. He ran back to the garage, looked at JoAnn Wilson lying on the garage floor, then dashed across the street to the house on the south side of 20th Avenue. For about thirty seconds he pounded frantically on the back door, yelling for help. There was no answer. By now, Dotson was panicking.

Inside the Wilson house things were peaceful. No one had heard anything of what had just happened in the garage.

11

Dotson raced through the Wilsons' back gate and up to the back of the house, where he knocked loudly on the glass doors, startling Maria. Following Dotson out to the garage, Maria burst into sobs when she saw JoAnn's body. Accompanied by Dotson, she returned to the house, where she stood in the kitchen, crying and screaming for Tony to come downstairs.

Upstairs, Wilson sprang from his bed and threw a dressing gown on. He ran quickly into the kitchen, where he found a panicky Dotson. Together the two men walked back out to the garage.

Wilson knelt beside the body for a moment, then jumped up and ran back into the house with Dotson on his heels. After phoning the police, Wilson silently went back to his wife's body. A bathrobe was his only protection from the frigid night air. In his haste, he'd forgotten even to put on slippers.

Wilson knelt beside the body, his bare legs and feet on the cold garage floor. He stayed quietly in place for several minutes, staring at the body of the woman he loved. On January 3, they had celebrated their second wedding anniversary.

JoAnn and Tony had a good marriage. They were determined to make it work, despite the continuous problems that Thatcher caused them. They had desperately hoped that after the property settlement and the custody battle were resolved Thatcher would leave them alone.

They may have suspected that something like this would happen. Only nineteen months earlier, in May 1981, JoAnn had been shot in the shoulder while standing in the kitchen doing the dishes. Life for the Wilsons had been terror-filled around that time, with harassing phone calls, slashed tires and sugar found in gas tanks.

Right after the wounding, Tony had negotiated the final property settlement for JoAnn. Prior to the shooting, the court had awarded Thatcher's ex-wife $819,000, one of the largest divorce settlements in Canadian history. After the shooting, that amount was reduced to $500,000. There had been no doubt in Tony and JoAnn's minds that the shooting was a tactic of Colin's designed to force a settlement in the divorce case.

Later, the Wilsons also decided to give up all attempts to maintain custody of Regan, JoAnn and Colin's second son. They hoped that Colin would be satisfied with that and would leave them to live their lives in peace. They made plans, they took holidays, they talked about how good it would be to have Regan living with them. JoAnn never entirely gave up hope that the boy would eventually be returned to her. In the meantime, they tried to give little Stephanie a normal life after the trauma of her parents' divorce.

JoAnn's murder had come only weeks before Colin was to pay the first instalment of $87,500 on the divorce settlement. The contract was written with a clause stipulating that if one person died the next payment was deferred for twelve months.

Wilson continued to kneel in anguish beside JoAnn. Dotson, who had silently placed himself a few feet behind Wilson, now stepped forward, removed his parka and slipped it over the shoulders of the grieving man. A few seconds later, Wilson got up and went back into the house to phone the police again.

Only a few minutes had passed. After the second call to the police, a car arrived almost immediately. It was 6:05 p.m., roughly only six minutes since Craig Dotson had passed the house and JoAnn had driven her car into the garage.

It was a tragic end to the love story of Colin and JoAnn, a story that had started full of hope and promise twenty-two years before in the small college town of Ames, Iowa. The marriage vows of "till death do us part" became a bitter reality for JoAnn on that cold

13

winter night in Regina, Saskatchewan, hundreds of miles from her home town.

The Thatchers' tumultuous marriage ended in adultery, threats and accusations of beatings and — the supreme violence — murder. The marriage was a life sentence for both of them. JoAnn's "term" ended on January 21, 1983. Colin didn't begin to serve his sentence until some fifteen months later, when he was arrested and charged with her murder.

Currently serving a life sentence with no possibility of parole for twenty-five years, he has recently launched an appeal.

CHAPTER TWO

Beginnings

Wilbert Colin Thatcher was born on August 25, 1938, in Toronto, Ontario. He is the only son of Wilbert Ross and Adra L. (Peggy) Thatcher.

Colin's father was born in 1917 in the small village of Neville, Saskatchewan. Ross Thatcher grew into an imposing, wealthy, powerful, articulate and intelligent politician and was probably the greatest single influence on Colin's life.

Ross went to a small country school until he was eleven, when his father moved the family to Moose Jaw and started a small hardware store. Ross later went to Queen's University, graduated at eighteen with a commerce degree and within a few years was assistant to the president of Canada Packers in Toronto. While he was working at Canada Packers, Ross married Peggy McNaughton—a pretty and gracious woman —the daughter of English immigrants. Colin was born shortly after, while the couple were still in Toronto.

The lure of the west was strong, however, and the family soon moved back to Saskatchewan, where Ross felt closer to his roots. In a short time, Ross took over the family hardware store and showed a keen eye for the business. Under his guidance, the enterprise branched out to include a second store in Moose Jaw and others in Saskatoon and Regina. While he was building his business, the senior Thatcher was also eyeing a career in politics. At age twenty-five he was a successful aldermanic candidate in the city for a two-year term; and, in 1945, running as a CCF candidate, he easily defeated the federal Liberal incumbent for the Moose Jaw riding.

When Ross went to the nation's capital, initially his family went with him, and Colin spent two years in a public school in Ottawa. Although Ross was to run successfully for the riding in 1949 and 1953, Colin continued his education in the Moose Jaw area. In 1955, Ross Thatcher left the CCF party and sat as an independent until the 1957 federal election. Peggy and Colin divided their time between Moose Jaw and Ottawa, and while in Moose Jaw, Peggy attended to her husband's constituency.

Colin was aware quite early in life that his family was special and, perhaps because of that, became rather arrogant. That arrogance eventually led him to believe that while he might be a lawmaker, he need not necessarily always obey the law himself.

Colin and his father didn't get along particularly well. Many years later, Colin would confide to his girlfriend, Lynne Dally (now Mendell), that his dad was verbally very abusive to him. "He would just yell and scream at Colin," Lynne says Colin told her. "Calling him names like 'good-for-nothing jerk'."

Those stories still circulate in Saskatchewan today. Ross would joke and laugh at the boy, and tell him he was stupid, in front of the farm hands. Mendell says Colin told her that Ross was not much different with Peggy, and that he often intimidated her, too. There were long periods of time when the boy didn't see his father, since the train was the main means of travel between Ottawa and Saskatchewan, and politicians didn't return home for weekends. Thus, Colin spent many of his early years under the influence of his mother.

When Ross was defeated as the federal Liberal candidate in 1957 and 1958, he became very involved with provincial politics. In 1959, he became the leader of the Saskatchewan Liberal Party and stayed with it until he was elected to power in 1964. The Thatchers then became the province's first family, with Peggy more than adequately filling the first lady's shoes. Today, she is respected and liked by almost everyone who knows her.

Ross, on the other hand, was a different story. It is fairly commonly held that he could be exceptionally hard on people. During cabinet meetings, he was known to reduce his ministers to tears in front of their colleagues, simply through a vicious tongue-lashing. This didn't hamper his political performance, however. By 1967, Ross Thatcher had boosted Liberal support in the province to thirty-five seats in a fifty-nine-seat legislature. He enjoyed his success until 1971 when Allan Blakeney and the NDP came to power.

At the same time that he entered provincial politics, Ross also branched out into farming, hoping to repeat his success with the hardware business in his agricultural operation. What started out as a few acres and a few head of cattle, Colin would eventually turn into an empire that was only half-jokingly called the "Dallas of the North". Colin would also receive the nickname of "the J.R. Ewing of Saskatchewan".

Ross's relationship with his son was never a close or warm one. Ross's authoritarian ways caused a coldness between father and son that many people believe partly accounts for Colin's hair-trigger temper and his quick and acerbic wit. Colin, like all young boys, wanted to be liked and accepted by his father. In his career, he eventually would follow in his father's footsteps to a large extent.

Despite his faults, Ross was well-respected in the province. He had helped strengthen the Liberal Party fortunes and was a power in that party for more than a decade.

17

His defeat in 1971 was more than he could handle. Ross was a diabetic who had suffered a stroke in 1969 — a fact very carefully hidden from the public by his family. Neither his son nor his daughter-in-law was particularly surprised when he passed away.

Ross Thatcher died shortly after his government was defeated in 1971. A doctor had warned him he was playing with fire by entering the election to begin with, but Ross thought his party was firmly entrenched. He was devastated by the defeat. No autopsy was ever done to determine the cause of death.

After his father's death, Colin developed a hatred of the NDP that has never abated. In the 1982 election the NDP was reduced to a rump party, with nine out of sixty-four seats. It's an understatement to say that Colin wasn't the slightest bit unhappy. "Seeing the NDP today clustered in one little corner of the Legislature, my goal in politics has been completed," Colin was quoted as saying, the day the House opened. "And I plan to do whatever I can to contribute to keeping them in that clustered corner."

Whatever his father's influence, Colin grew into a powerful man in his own right. He's intelligent, well-educated, born to money and power, witty and downright charming, when he wants to be. At just over six feet tall, with dark hair and blue eyes, he had no trouble attracting women and developed a particular liking for blondes.

He and JoAnn Kay Geiger hit it off on their first date, in the spring of 1960.

JoAnn was born on August 21, 1939, in Osage, Iowa, to Harlan and Betty Geiger. She had an older brother, Don, who's now a businessman. Two younger sisters followed: Carolyn, now a teacher, and Nancy, a librarian.

The family moved to Ames, Iowa, in 1945. It's a quiet college town where more than half the population are students. Harlan, for a while an associate professor at Iowa State University, later became a county government worker in the agricultural extension field. Betty had studied home economics at the university.

JoAnn was a pretty girl, with brown eyes and blonde curls. She wasn't sports-minded, but instead preferred such domestic and traditionally feminine pursuits as cooking and fashion. She had a solid Methodist upbringing in a family-oriented home.

She grew into a lovely teenager with an attractive, appealing personality that helped her make friends easily. She was gregarious, independent, strong-willed, proud, kind, warm and loving. She loved dancing and entertaining. There were no steady boyfriends for JoAnn in high school; she preferred group activities, going to parties and dances with her friends. She never lacked a date on these occasions; it was simply that there was no one who was particularly special.

JoAnn graduated from high school at the top of her class. At first, she planned to go away to school, but later changed her mind and enrolled in home economics at Iowa State, like her mother before her.

She was an artistic young woman, who displayed a flair for designing. She also sewed most of her own clothes. Eventually, she decided she would like to be a buyer for a large department store. She did so well in her marketing courses that she was offered a summer job at a large store in St. Louis. Because of her flair for fashion and design, her parents thought she would probably end up working in a big city.

JoAnn was both a hard worker — she had had several part-time jobs during high school — and very well liked. Everyone who remembers JoAnn has nothing but nice things to say about her. She had "class".

"JoAnn was the type of woman you married and had children with," Colin said many years later.

JoAnn and Colin met in their last year of university.

19

Colin was sitting in the school union office one after-noon, about three months before his graduation, when an attractive blonde girl walked by. She piqued his interest, so he asked one of his friends who she was. The answer came: JoAnn Geiger. In those days, blind dates on campus weren't uncommon, so Colin phoned JoAnn and asked her out for a date that Saturday night.

When he arrived to pick her up, there was no sign of the woman he had seen in the office. A different girl approached him and said, ''Hello Colin,'' but Colin didn't pay much attention. JoAnn said ''Hello'' again, and that's when Thatcher realized there had been a mix-up, that he had been given the wrong name.

They went out that Saturday night anyway. She was twenty; he was twenty-one. It wasn't long before they started to go steady, and later that spring Colin asked JoAnn to wear his fraternity pin — the traditional sign that they were engaged to be engaged. Neither of them was exactly certain where the relationship was going, because Colin was scheduled to complete his bachelor of science degree that spring. But they continued to see each other constantly, up until his graduation.

Colin met JoAnn's parents that spring for the first time. JoAnn invited him for Easter dinner and told her mother that he was something special, and that they were pinned. JoAnn had never had a serious boy-friend before. ''There was one young man in south-west Iowa,'' Harlan recalls. ''He talked her into visit-ing his parents. He was more serious about her than she was about him.''

That Easter dinner the Geigers met — and liked — their future son-in-law. ''He seemed perfectly nice,'' Harlan says. ''He can put on a real nice appearance.''

The Geigers only had to look at JoAnn to realize how happy she was with her young Canadian rancher. Colin and Harlan had a lot in common, since they both had strong agricultural interests, and it was easy for the two men to talk.

Even then, however, Harlan was a little distressed by some of the stories Colin told him. "He was inclined to take things into his own hands," the professor remembers.

Colin had told him a story about finding a car parked on his land that probably belonged to some poachers. "He told me he just pointed his shotgun and fired two shots through the radiator," Geiger said.

That story bothered Harlan because Colin didn't seem to have acted with much common sense; Geiger didn't care for the way the young man had chosen to resolve the situation.

That summer JoAnn went to Moose Jaw—her future home — for a visit. On the eve of her twenty-first birthday, Colin was thrown by a horse, and it looked as though he might lose the use of one arm. He decided to return to Iowa State for another year and take his master's degree in animal husbandry while he recovered from the accident.

At Christmas, JoAnn returned again to Moose Jaw, and the young couple decided they would be married. When JoAnn went back to school after the break she switched some of her courses so she could qualify as a teacher. There wouldn't be much call for her marketing skills in Moose Jaw.

The couple were married on August 12, 1962. They were very much in love, and it was plain to see that it was the happiest day in JoAnn's young life. She walked down the aisle of the Ames Methodist Church exactly nine days before her twenty-third birthday. Her new husband was twenty-four.

The pictures of their wedding show an exuberant, hopeful young couple. They had everything to look forward to. They were young, healthy, well-educated.

21

Ross and Peggy, who had taken to JoAnn from the beginning and were delighted with the match, travelled down to Iowa to attend the wedding.

Harlan remembers an odd comment of Ross's on the day after the wedding. JoAnn had gone to pack the wedding gifts; Colin was upstairs reading. "I sure hope Jo can handle him," Ross told the Geigers, "because we never could."

At the time, Harlan didn't attach too much significance to Ross's words, because Ross sort of laughed when he spoke. But Geiger was to remember the remark clearly more than two decades later.

Colin didn't go out of his way to ingratiate himself with his new in-laws. The wedding was the last time he went to their home until 1979, when he wanted to find his wife. The Geigers never understood his evident indifference, since they had always treated Colin very well.

JoAnn and Colin moved to Moose Jaw and settled into an apartment in a building owned by Ross. JoAnn taught high school and Colin ran the ranch on a full-time basis as well as helping Ross with his political career. The marriage was off to a good start. One of the first things Colin did was buy JoAnn a golden horse, something she had always wanted.

The Geigers were glad to hear that the young couple was happy, because Harlan had real reservations about his new son-in-law. He feared his violent tempers.

JoAnn didn't care all that much for teaching, but she was conscientious and did a good job. And the young couple's social life developed. Colin and JoAnn started spending a lot of time with Colin's old friend Ron Graham and his wife, Jane. Ron and Colin had known each other since grade two. The two couples had dinner together frequently, played cards and took vacations together. They both started their families at about the same time.

JoAnn became pregnant around Thanksgiving in 1964. On June 26 of the following year she gave birth to Gregory Ross Thatcher. There weren't two prouder or happier parents in the world. The new grandson was a delight to Ross, who spoiled young Greg rotten.

Also in 1964, Ross became premier. When he moved to Regina he sold the family home on 1116 Redland Avenue to Colin for $7,500, much less than its market value of $25,000. It was the only home the Thatcher children would know. An imposing-looking house with large trees in the front yard and steps leading up to the front door, it had four bedrooms and a bathroom upstairs; downstairs were the formal dining room, living room and kitchen. The den was a later addition to the house. Because green was JoAnn's favourite colour, the outside and much of the interior were painted green.

With the birth of her son, JoAnn stopped working outside the home and gave all her attention to the family. The ranching and farming businesses were growing and JoAnn took book-keeping courses so she could help Colin keep the business in order. She continued to enjoy a good relationship with her in-laws. Ross doted on her, and in return she became very active in his campaigning and helped entertain political friends. She and Peggy often went shopping together, sometimes taking trips to New York City.

The young couple were to wait a while before more children followed. JoAnn had a difficult time between Greg's birth and her next child. Twice she became pregnant and twice she miscarried. One of these unsuccessful pregnancies was particularly bad because JoAnn and Colin found out at three months that the baby was dead and had to wait another three months until it miscarried.

In 1969, on February 19, a second child, Regan Colin Thatcher, was born. Colin was delighted with the new addition to the family. Sons would carry on the Thatcher name and business.

On January 7, 1974, the arrival of Stephanie Ann completed the family. Of the three children, she was most like her mother.

To outsiders, the Thatcher household appeared to be a happy one. The business was going well, the children were healthy, bright and attractive, and both Colin and JoAnn were active in the community. Colin belonged to the Kinsmen's Club and coached a midget hockey team. JoAnn was busy making and keeping their house a comfortable, warm and loving place. Only those close to the Thatchers knew that the marriage was beginning to develop cracks that would eventually bring it tumbling down.

CHAPTER THREE

A Marriage Crumbles

The Geigers knew from quite early on that there was something amiss in their oldest daughter's marriage. Not on their first visit to Moose Jaw, though. During that stay, Colin was polite and attentive to them, spending time with Harlan and showing him around the family spread. "He seemed proud of what he had and proud of what he was doing," Harlan remembers.

At first, the Geigers were prepared to make the 1,700 kilometre drive every year, but gradually, as the years went by, they began to see changes, particularly after the children started arriving. The visits seemed to become more and more tense. "Later on, we felt he was being hard on the kids and putting Jo down just to needle us," Harlan said.

The Geigers started to break up their trips, spending the first day in Moose Jaw, going on to Prince Albert or Jasper for the middle part of the vacation and stopping in Moose Jaw again on their way home.

Harlan said that Colin paid little attention to the children; when he did notice them, as often as not it was to bawl them out, usually for something minor like walking in front of the television while he was trying to watch it.

They also noticed a disturbing tenseness in their daughter, but JoAnn did not discuss her marriage with them. "She wasn't one to talk," Harlan says. It wasn't until years later that they realized how bad the situation was.

JoAnn would apologize for her husband's behaviour. She would sometimes make excuses for him, saying that he wasn't normally like that, and that he did take good care of them.

As the visits got shorter and less frequent, the Geigers noticed that Thatcher seemed to put Jo down a lot in front of them, which bothered them a great deal. Eventually, by 1976, the Geigers stopped visiting. They felt their presence put an extra strain on JoAnn and the grandchildren that they could do without. Instead, JoAnn tried to get down to visit, bringing the children with her. The Geigers were particularly delighted with Stephanie. "She's almost so smart she scares you," Harlan says of the little girl. "I remember once JoAnn telling us she didn't want Colin to know how smart she was in case he was too hard on her when she did make a mistake."

Harlan is quick to point out that the children inherited a lot of their intelligence from Colin, who is unquestionably a bright man. "You can't belittle Colin in terms of smarts," Geiger says.

After Ross died in 1971, Thatcher really threw himself into expanding the family business. He had inherited his father's financial acumen and now he set out to build an agricultural empire that would eventually make him one of the biggest landowners in Saskatchewan. Through the 1970s he increased his ranch herds of registered Simmentals and Herefords, as well as maintaining his profitable grain operation.

He acquired a three-bedroom condominium in Palm Springs, California. By his own admission, that became his playground after JoAnn left him. He also owned an interest in a cable-television operation in Moose Jaw.

The Thatcher empire is on shaky ground today. The recession in the early 1980s caused beef prices to plummet, and Thatcher admits to having cash-flow

26

problems. The massive marriage settlement he was initially ordered to pay JoAnn would have forced him to sell off his valuable lands, although the reduced settlement gave him a little more breathing space. At the time of the trial, however, Tony Wilson was still trying to get the remainder of the money owing to JoAnn's estate from Thatcher. Most of that money is supposed to be paid into a trust for Stephanie. Thatcher has also admitted that several financial institutions are currently after him for money.

After his father's death, Colin leaped into the political fray. He sought the Liberal nomination in Ross's own riding, but ended up getting massacred. He tried again in 1974, and this time won the party's nod for the riding of Thunder Creek. It's a huge constituency, which sits like a rectangle around the outside of Moose Jaw. Colin related well to his constituents because they, like him, made a living off the land. He understood their concerns and gave them good representation in the House.

In 1976, Thatcher briefly considered running for the Liberal leadership, but decided against it. He had struck up a friendship with the Progressive Conservative leader, Dick Collver, and, in 1977, seeing his own party's fortunes decline, joined his Liberal colleague, Gary Lane (the provincial attorney general at the time of Thatcher's arrest), in crossing the floor to join the PCs.

Thatcher's bolt from his father's party threw the House into confusion over which party would have Official Opposition status. The NDP held thirty-nine seats, while the Liberals and PCs were tied at eleven after Thatcher's move.

One reason Thatcher gave for the move was that the provincial Liberals were too closely tied to their federal counterparts. Both Colin and his father had been critical of the federal Liberals who, Colin felt, dominated their provincial counterparts. Also, he felt that the Progressive Conservatives had a better chance of winning the next provincial election, and he wanted to belong to the party in power to help move the province back to what he called "a common-sense" government. The PCs were defeated in 1978, but rode to power in 1982 under the guidance of Grant Devine.

While Colin's political career was getting off the ground, JoAnn was a willing assistant and supporter. She worked hard, happily knocking on doors, giving coffee parties and attending rallies.

But the marriage was falling apart. In the first affidavit JoAnn filed for divorce in 1979, she indicated that the problems had started in 1977, when Thatcher first started treating her badly.

"My husband started coming home frequently at 2:30 to 3 a.m., and when I tried to speak to him concerning the matter, he told me that if I did not like it I knew what I could do; and in addition, the respondent was belligerent towards me, and on two occasions he struck me with his fist, which resulted in a black eye on each occasion; and on a further occasion he accused me of giving him venereal disease," she wrote.

One of JoAnn's girlfriends later filed an affidavit saying she had seen Jo with black eyes, and that Jo had told her that Colin was responsible. JoAnn was quite stoical about the beatings, choosing to wear sunglasses to prevent people from knowing about the problem.

Colin's version of events is decidedly different. "I did not frequently begin to come home at 2:30 or 3:00 in the morning; when the Legislature is in session it often sits nights until 10:00, and sometimes I would spend time with caucus members or members of the press after the House adjourned; but even taking into account those occasions, I certainly was not out frequently until 2:30 or 3:00 and we did not have discussion where I implied to my wife that she should get out of the house; in fact our relationship hadn't reached a point where there was a discussion of separation,'' Colin said.

He categorically denied hitting JoAnn at any time. According to Thatcher, the black eyes happened accidentally during their discussion about venereal disease. He said they were talking in bed about it and started to argue. When he turned over in bed quickly, he caught her on the bridge of the nose with his elbow. ''It was accidental, even though I was turning in anger. I certainly did not intend to strike her — I felt very badly about striking her,'' he said.

That's a different explanation from the one he gave in his testimony at the trial, when he said that JoAnn got the black eyes when he fell off a ladder accidentally and struck her in the face with his elbow as he tumbled. His affidavit explains the rest of the story.

''It is true that I accused my wife of giving me venereal disease and I am embarrassed that I made that accusation to her. I had broken out with an infection. I thought it was venereal disease. I did not want to go to a doctor and was embarrassed. I had had the infection for some days. I was out one evening and had a few drinks and when I came back I sat on the bed and accused my wife of giving me venereal disease. I knew that if I had venereal disease, I had to have caught it from her. She said that she had not slept with anyone and that if I had venereal disease I had caught it from someone else, and that it therefore was not venereal disease and I should go to a doctor. I then went to a doctor and found that it was an infection that was not in any way a result of sexual contact,'' Colin wrote.

That incident happened in 1978 and the marriage was damaged beyond repair. Harlan Geiger says there was one remark that cut JoAnn's heart in two — the comment that if she didn't like it, she knew what she could do.

"It hurt JoAnn so much when he said that," Harlan said. "She knew it didn't matter then."

JoAnn had begun to hear of her husband's infidelities from Ron Graham, Colin's best friend. JoAnn was doing some work for Graham's construction company when the trouble in the marriage started. She had opened a small design business, and Graham had asked her to do some work on new offices in Vancouver and Edmonton. Graham had phoned Colin to ask if he minded JoAnn's accompanying him. Colin says now that he was delighted. He had been worried about JoAnn, he says, because she seemed very unhappy. She wasn't sleeping and she was losing weight. "It wasn't unusual to find her crying and sobbing," Thatcher said, adding, "I don't mean to suggest I was a perfect husband. At times I was all too average."

The way Colin was acting around the house might have been partly responsible for JoAnn's tears. In the same affidavit in which she outlined the beatings, she revealed some of the problems in their home life. "During the course of our marriage, my husband was frequently away from home, [and] was often distant and cold in his relations with our children, to the point [where] the children frequently avoided him," she wrote.

"My husband's attitude towards the children was frequently surly and moody and on occasion, in a display of temper, he would smash a glass against the wall or the kitchen cupboards.

"My husband has become abrasive and has isolated himself from relatives and friends and I am fearful that my children are not obtaining any normal interrelationships with other people but are being isolated in their own home," she concluded.

That was a sentiment she was later to echo to her

parents. Harlan said that JoAnn didn't want her children growing up in that atmosphere and that she feared it might damage them psychologically. She wanted to give them a good home, and felt she had to leave the marriage for their well-being as well as her own.

Colin denied JoAnn's allegations, saying that the ones relating to the children were "ridiculous". He added that the children had numerous friends who were always welcome in their home.

Another factor undermining the crumbling marriage was the adultery on both sides. Graham had told JoAnn about Colin's infidelities. Now she, too, began to be unfaithful — with Colin's best friend.

The business trip for the design business had led to something more. What had started out as a business dinner led to a brief affair. But JoAnn's father says that the affair only occurred after JoAnn knew the marriage was hopelessly broken down.

"Ron told her that he wanted to get a divorce and marry her, but she sensed that maybe that wasn't going to happen," her dad remembers. He added that after a while other people entered into it and plans changed. But JoAnn had made up her mind to leave Colin no matter what, he claims. The situation with Ron didn't influence her decision in any way.

Apparently Colin did not at first know of the affair. But someone else did; that person was Jane Graham, Ron's wife. It was Jane who told Colin about the affair, in 1978. At first, Colin says, he didn't believe her. "I asked JoAnn and she convinced me it was ridiculous," he said. That conversation happened in the fall of 1978.

In the spring of 1979, Jane Graham repeated the accusation, after the Grahams had been at the Thatchers' house for dinner. "I told her, 'You're crazy and you're paranoid,' " Colin says. Thatcher learned about the infidelity mostly through the court appearances in the divorce proceedings, where JoAnn testified under oath.

"He [Ron] would call at strange times, ostensibly for me, but it seemed to me to be times when he should not have expected me to be home; his wife kept telling me that they had a relationship but I kept telling her that I thought she was wrong and I couldn't believe it," Colin later wrote in an affidavit.

There were other problems in the relationship, too. JoAnn didn't like Moose Jaw and yearned for the big city. "I started hearing things like, 'If we stay here, Stephanie will probably marry somebody from this country,' " Colin recalls.

"I would frequently find my wife crying and when I would try to comfort her, she would say that she was rotting in Moose Jaw and that she had to get out, and that it had been a mistake for her to have come to Moose Jaw in the first place. She would tell me that she should not have left the work force and given up her career," Thatcher reported in his initial affidavit.

Colin insists that in the last eight months of the marriage he treated JoAnn better than he ever had. That may well have been true, but it must have been a case of too little too late. By the early summer of 1979, JoAnn had made up her mind definitely that she was leaving Colin. The tempers and the scenes had become too much for her. She wanted a different life for herself and her children.

There is one trait that Colin and JoAnn had in common: their stubbornness. The course on which she was about to embark embroiled JoAnn in scandal, insult, shame and violence. Although she knew it wasn't going to be easy, she felt in her heart of hearts that she was doing the right thing. We shall never know if she would have acted differently had she suspected the true horror of what lay ahead.

CHAPTER FOUR

Breaking Free

On August 12, 1979, JoAnn packed up Stephanie and Regan and made her escape. It was seventeen years to the day since she and Colin had exchanged wedding vows in Ames, Iowa.

She had carefully timed her departure to coincide with Colin's absence on a five-day bachelor holiday with his best friend (and JoAnn's lover), Ron Graham. The vacation was supposed to provide the two businessmen with a little golf and a little sun.

Colin had planned to take JoAnn out for an anniversary dinner when he returned from Palm Springs. He later said that JoAnn had insisted he take the trip, but that is unlikely, since he was accompanied on his golfing excursion by a young woman. That woman was twenty-four-year-old Janice Gardiner from Estevan, Saskatchewan. Colin sandwiched his golf games in between his indoor activities with Gardiner. (Later Gardiner was a co-respondent in the divorce case.)

Ron Graham cut his holiday short by a day, asking Thatcher to drive him to the airport. From there, Colin spoke briefly to JoAnn on the phone. It was a normal conversation, probably because JoAnn was petrified that Colin would suspect her plans. She knew his temper and his reactions intimately and knew she could never depart peacefully with his children.

On the following day — their wedding anniversary — Thatcher tore himself away from Gardiner long enough to phone home. When Greg answered and said that JoAnn had taken the two youngest children somewhere, Colin instantly suspected that something was wrong. Greg had just turned fourteen, and JoAnn had left him in the care of Blaine Matheson, the boyfriend of Sandra Hammond (later Silversides).

JoAnn didn't take Greg with her primarily because she knew he wouldn't go. Greg had become very close to his father, and very much like him. Also, Greg had started to show a great deal of interest in his father's farming and ranching operations, and she knew he would prefer to stay. However, JoAnn harboured the hope that eventually, when the family settled down, Greg would want to join his brother and sister.

Colin flew back to Regina and went on to Moose Jaw, where he spent the evening waiting for JoAnn to call.

"That evening I was sitting there, something just made me go upstairs and look in her closet, and then I knew," he said. "Her closet was empty."

Thatcher immediately phoned his mother, Peggy, but she had no idea what was happening because JoAnn hadn't told her anything. Next, Colin tried Graham, in the hope that he had returned from Texas. A short time later, Jane Graham showed up at the house. She walked in the door and stood silhouetted by the streetlight. Thatcher was sitting just inside. He said he'd never forget the conversation.

"She's in Texas with my husband," Jane said. "I told you before they were having an affair. She's with my husband in Texas."

Thatcher's massive ego wouldn't allow him to believe the truth. He yelled at Jane that it wasn't true and that he didn't believe her.

The next day, Ron Graham called. He expressed shock and disbelief that JoAnn was gone, as well as sympathy. Thatcher assumed that Graham was calling from Texas, but in fact the man was in Brampton, Ontario, with JoAnn and the two children. It was deception in the extreme.

Thatcher began to write torrid love letters to JoAnn, which he sent to her through an intermediary. Those love letters later became exhibits at the divorce trial. They expressed passion and love for JoAnn, literally begging her to come home.

Thatcher was exhibiting the signs of a classic wife-beater, men who are miserable to live with but fall apart when the object of their abuse packs up and leaves. Thatcher was stunned. He couldn't believe JoAnn had left him.

The three love letters, written on consecutive days, are in Thatcher's own handwriting on official sta-tionery for the Province of Saskatchewan's Legisla-tive Assembly.

8/18

My dearest JoAnn:

Words cannot describe the agony, emptiness and grief inside me. Greg figured things out yesterday and he is heartbroken. I almost break down every time I look at him.

I beg you to communicate with me by phone. It is the not knowing that is so terribly difficult. I cannot eat, I cannot sleep, I cannot go very far in case you should phone. Life has no meaning with-out you. You are my love and I will always love you. I beg you not to do this to our kids. Greg's face tells it all.

I am too grief-stricken to be angry at your actions. I blame myself for being so intransigent about your desire for seclusion. I respect the manner in which you have withdrawn to your seclusion.

I pray your reflections will cause you to decide to return to us. I have no terms or conditions — only an insatiable desire for you and the kids.

I have many questions about Stephanie and Regan. Please allow me to ask them soon.

I have always respected you. Your actions in this case have increased this respect. You have done it with class. I know that you, too, hurt inside and feel much the same way I do. I cannot imagine a life without you and the kids. *Please come home*. We both love you and need you.

Love,
Colin

8/19

My dearest Jo:

I am writing this second letter because Jack is away until tomorrow and I cannot get it mailed until his return. It feels so strange to communicate in this fashion.

I deserve what you have done. Since I can do nothing except feel sorry for myself, by necessity I have also been reflecting. I feel guilty about many things, especially for the poor quality husband I have been for the vast majority of 17 years.

However, I do feel I have been a good husband and father this past year. You have been a marvellous wife for 16 of our 17 years.

I again ask you to consider the positive aspects of our marriage, and there have been many. I have learned a lesson from this experience — a lesson I feel would be helpful in continuing our marriage.

While I yearn to know your plans and talk to the kids, I know better than to interfere with your seclusion. Even if I knew your whereabouts, I would not come. I miss you all so desperately. I *have* learned from this.

Come home,
love
Colin

My darling Jo:

Time passes so slowly. It is terrible to wake up wishing this day was over.

Our son has become a man. I am amazed at the manner he has matured these past few days. I am very proud of him.

As I am proud of Greg, I ache for Stephanie and Regan. For their mother, I would pay any price to have her back.

A death in the family would be easier to handle than this. Still, I take all the blame for my intransigence in forcing this course of action upon you.

It is most repetitive in saying "I love you and need you." The lessons of this experience have given those words a much broader dimension than they have ever meant.

Please come home.
Love
Colin

But even the letters couldn't bring a phone call from JoAnn. The line about a death in the family may have been a little too close to the bone for her. It has a grim irony, in retrospect.

Ron Graham returned to town a few days later. By this time Thatcher had come to believe the truth about JoAnn and Ron. A scene followed a short time later on the golf-course green. Thatcher waited until the fourth hole to speak his mind. Then he told Graham he was going to get the "embarrassment of his life" if he didn't tell Thatcher where his family was by the time the final putt was sunk. Graham sheepishly said he'd try to arrange a phone call. Thatcher was extremely bitter about his best friend's betrayal.

JoAnn phoned the next day. Thatcher suspected she

was in Ames, Iowa, with her family. He and Greg immediately drove straight down there.

The Geigers were polite but very cool. JoAnn had been there, but Colin had missed her by about a day. She was on her way to Brampton where she was going to start her new life. Since leaving Colin, she and the children had travelled a bit. They'd been to Brampton and to Iowa, and had spent some time in Texas with Ron Graham. Now JoAnn had purchased a house and enrolled in a course at Ryerson Polytechnical Institute in Toronto. The children were registered in a Brampton school.

JoAnn had friends in Brampton. The Reverend John Sullivan and his wife, Marilee, had been the incumbents at the United Church in Moose Jaw for some time. JoAnn had become close to them; indeed, she stayed with them in Brampton until she got settled in the house that Ron Graham helped her acquire.

By this time, JoAnn had phoned Colin several times just to let him know she and the children were all right. He was doing everything he possibly could to entice her to come back, but she was having no part of it.

Colin got a lucky break in his search at this point. Jane Graham had rifled her husband's pockets and come up with a phone number. It had no area code, but Thatcher dialled the Toronto prefix, and when JoAnn answered he knew he had the right number. From the phone number, he secured an address and was on his way to Brampton.

Colin had duped JoAnn. When she phoned him on September 7 to tell him the children were fine and enrolled in school, he told her he had no intention of taking the kids away from her. The custody could wait until they worked out how they were going to approach the divorce. JoAnn said she was about to file the papers, but Colin asked her to hold off until he found a lawyer and could finish the fall harvest.

On September 11, Thatcher flew east and kidnapped the two children. He had enlisted the help of Sandra Hammond, who, at age eighteen, had been baby-sitting for the Thatchers for almost five years. Thatcher hired Hammond to be his part-time housekeeper/baby-sitter for the next two years while she was taking a light load at school. In the custody battle her presence in the home helped him prove that he could provide a stable environment for the children.

Thatcher later said, to the amazement of those who listened, that Sandra's mother, Beverly, paid him the greatest compliment of his life by trusting him, a forty-year-old man, with her eighteen-year-old daughter. For a man with a high-level political career and substantial business operations, it seemed an odd achievement to cite as the highest of his life.

On a street in Brampton, Colin and Sandra pulled up to Stephanie and Regan while they were on their way to school. Both children came running to the car and got in. They hadn't gone two blocks before Stephanie piped up: "We've been seeing a lot of Uncle Ron these days." From the children, Colin was able to piece together the extent of his betrayal. His heart began to harden towards JoAnn for the shame she was causing him.

Thatcher immediately took the children back to Moose Jaw, but waited until the next morning to phone JoAnn and tell her he had the children. He added that they were safe and well-guarded where JoAnn couldn't get at them.

JoAnn flew back to Moose Jaw and abandoned all attempts to live in the east. She tried to contact Stephanie at the King George School, where she was enrolled, but was told by the school authorities that Stephanie was not to be released from the school until an authorized person picked her up. JoAnn was not authorized. In her affidavit for custody of the children, JoAnn said

Thatcher had implied he'd be willing to sacrifice the children to her if she promised not to go after a property settlement. That, like many things that Thatcher said, was simply untrue. He had no intention of letting the children go to JoAnn. And he would fight to the bitter end for them.

The hatred that Colin came to feel for JoAnn was taking root in his soul. She shamed him when she cuckolded him. His ego couldn't take the fact that his wife — his *property* — had rejected him. There was a growing resolve inside Thatcher to make things as difficult as he could for her — to thwart her at every turn. He convinced himself that he was the wronged party in the marriage, that he had done nothing wrong and that he had been a good husband. The ungrateful bitch had simply thrown everything he had given her back in his face. He would never forgive her.

When JoAnn arrived back in Moose Jaw, Colin had already obtained an order for interim custody of the children until a full custody hearing could be arranged. In the interim, Mr. Justice J. A. MacPherson ruled that JoAnn could have access to the children on weekends, and that on those occasions Colin had to leave the house to allow her time alone with them.

Mr. Justice MacPherson was to play a large role in the Thatchers' lives during the months that followed. He heard all the custody proceedings and made the rulings on the homes for the children. The judge was to become very familiar with the intimate secrets of the marriage and separation, and he formed some very strong opinions about Colin's behaviour in the entire matter.

JoAnn waited it out in Moose Jaw until the custody hearing. She had no permanent place to stay and started a nomadic existence, which was to continue until the spring of the following year. She lived on stocks and bonds she had accumulated during the marriage. Colin wasn't giving her a cent.

JoAnn was bearing up well. She had many good friends who gave her the support and comfort she needed. One of them went so far as to file an affidavit in court to the effect that she had seen JoAnn with black eyes prior to her separation from Colin. JoAnn had been closed off from the outside world somewhat during the marriage. It wasn't until the separation that she realized how important her network of friends was.

Thatcher believed that JoAnn hated him for breaking her dream of living in Brampton. "I believed that JoAnn had gone to Brampton and she had intended to get her divorce as quickly as possible. She believed Graham would do likewise, and somewhere down the road she would be Mrs. Graham," Thatcher said. But that wasn't in the cards; Ron Graham continued to stay with Jane.

JoAnn was now trying to make the best of a bad situation. She had escaped from a terrible marriage, but was determined to maintain a relationship with her children. She went to the house every weekend to spend time with them.

It wasn't easy. Greg refused to stay in the same house with JoAnn. When JoAnn showed up for weekend visits, Greg would run to his grandmother's, a few blocks away, and stay there. Although he was only fourteen, he was strong-willed and had a temper. Colin had already begun poisoning the boy's mind against JoAnn. Greg's disaffection would later manifest itself in a sickening way.

One weekend, Colin did something that Mr. Justice MacPherson said was "unforgivable, tasteless and even mean". When JoAnn arrived for her usual weekend visit, on the refrigerator door, attached with a small kitchen magnet, was a neatly clipped newspaper article, about a man in Rhode Island who had sued a friend for having an affair with his wife. The large headline read: ''Man Ordered to Pay $80,000 for Affair with Friend's Wife.''

Colin testified at the custody hearing that he put the article there as a weak attempt at humour, but the judge didn't think it was very funny, and pointed out in his decision that Colin had deliberately put the clipping in a place where the boys as well as JoAnn could read it. ''Thus it was either a thoughtless or deliberate demeaning of the wife in her sons' immature minds,'' the judge said.

On November 27, 1979, after a two-day custody hearing, Mr. Justice MacPherson ruled that JoAnn would have custody of Stephanie and Regan while Greg would stay with his father.

In comparing JoAnn and Colin as parents, the judge found Colin lacking: ''I was less favourably impressed by the personality of the husband than I was with that of the wife. I accept the wife's testimony that he is moody, given to sudden tempers and occasionally to foul language. There are lots of good parents who are worse.

''There are several positive reasons for awarding custody of Regan and Stephanie to the wife. She is a much warmer, more affectionate and sympathetic person than the husband. I venture the thought that his lack of these qualities, his failure to appreciate the wife, caused the marriage breakdown. Adultery is rarely the cause, it is the result,'' the judge concluded.

Mr. Justice MacPherson pointed out that Colin was an adequate parent but, in simple terms, JoAnn was a better one. The judge also decided that JoAnn, as the mother, could give better care to Regan and Stephanie than Sandra Hammond or any competent housekeeper.

He added that he hoped time would teach Greg that

he could demonstrate a natural affection for JoAnn without being disloyal to Colin. "He must be encouraged by both parents to visit Regan and Stephanie in his mother's home," the judge said.

He concluded the hearing by saying that both Colin and JoAnn were to have access to the children "at all reasonable times" and that neither parent was to take the children out of the area without the other's consent in writing. And he ordered Colin to pay JoAnn's legal fees.

That custody order was never to take effect. Colin discussed the situation with his divorce lawyer, Tony Merchant, and they decided to appeal. Merchant, a lawyer and a well-known Saskatchewan Liberal, had been an acquaintance of Thatcher's for twenty years. The pair became friendly when they were both sitting MLAs between 1975 and 1978. Merchant was to play a key role in the drama that unfolded in the next few years.

Once the appeal was launched, the situation was frozen. JoAnn never took custody of the children and she continued to visit on weekends while she stayed at the home of friends.

At Christmas, Colin took all three children with him to Palm Springs. Thatcher said JoAnn was within a hair of deciding to join them. He was so certain about this that he had ordered an extra airplane ticket for her. When she decided not to go, he turned the ticket over to Blaine Matheson, Sandra's boyfriend.

Thatcher was still actively pursuing a reconciliation with JoAnn. Whether he wanted her back because he genuinely loved her or just because he wanted to torment her with her infidelity is not known. In any case, he enlisted the help of his old political buddy, Dick Collver, to act as an intermediary with JoAnn. Collver readily agreed and arranged for JoAnn to have dinner with him and his wife, Eleanor. Colin had asked Dick

43

to convince JoAnn to go home where she belonged.

During the meal, Dick brought the subject up, but JoAnn adamantly refused even to entertain the idea. "I am afraid, afraid for myself and afraid for my children," she repeated over and over again that evening.

At one point during the meal she excused herself and went to the washroom. When she returned to the table she said she wasn't feeling well and asked to go home. Collver and his wife concluded that the thought of returning to a life with Colin was enough to make her ill with nervousness, so they diplomatically dropped the subject.

Collver reported to Colin that he should forget JoAnn and just get on with his life. To Dick's surprise, Colin refused to do that. He became obsessed with JoAnn. "He was obsessed with the problems he had," Collver recalls. "He couldn't think of politics or anything else."

To take Colin's mind off his marital problems, Collver invited him to bring his children to the Collver ranch in Arizona during the Christmas break. The ranch was only a few hours' drive from Thatcher's condominium in Palm Springs. Thatcher called Collver on Boxing Day and arrived at the ranch on December 28 with the three children, Sandra and Blaine.

It didn't take long for the Thatcher family to upset Dick and his wife. They were friends of JoAnn and very fond of her. To their horror, Colin and Sandra repeatedly referred to JoAnn as "the bitch" in front of the children.

"I must say I never heard Colin or the baby-sitter refer to JoAnn as anything other than 'the bitch'," Collver recalled of that visit. "It upset me and my wife because of the children. He was upset, now, remember; his best friend had run away with his wife, he was more than hurt, he was stabbed inside," Collver says in Thatcher's defence.

During the day, however, Collver discovered something even more distressing. Sandra and Blaine had somehow managed to get hold of a credit card that belonged to Ron Graham. They were teaching the three children to make long-distance calls all over the world on Graham's card. When Thatcher was informed about it, he merely laughed and did nothing to stop the game.

During that day, December 29, Collver says Thatcher approached him three different times with a grisly proposition. "I have only one solution for the bitch. The only solution is that I've got to hire somebody to kill her."

Thatcher knew Collver was friendly with a few defence lawyers who could easily put him in touch with some unsavoury characters, and he wanted Dick to do him the favour.

"I said, 'No, don't even talk to me about it. You're embarrassing me. You're going beyond friendship.' " Collver reported.

"I attempted through the course of the day on at least three different occasions to get rid of this obsession," Collver said. "I said, 'Colin, stop it. Get on with your life.' "

But it wasn't to be. Thatcher continued to demean JoAnn in front of his host and the children and he talked incessantly about killing her to Dick. Collver tried a final time at dinner that night to talk Thatcher out of his obsession, but gave up in disgust. He asked his guest to leave.

"Until you're rid of this obsession I'm going to ask you to leave my ranch. I don't want you here at this time," Collver said. Thatcher packed up the children and left the next morning.

The talk of a paid killer had truly upset Dick. He called his lawyer, although he didn't wish to become involved. Ron Barclay advised him he had no legal

45

obligation to do anything about the conversation. Dick tried to put it out of his mind and hoped it was merely a passing thought on Colin's part.

In the spring of 1980, Collver had one last embroilment in the divorce wrangles of Colin and JoAnn. Dick believed that by that time Colin was doing much better; he had never mentioned the idea of a paid killer again. On the night the Legislature opened in the spring, Thatcher approached Collver again and asked him to intervene in the property and custody settlements. Colin and JoAnn were becoming sick of the lawyers. Colin told Dick his bottom line to settle at was $400,000 and custody of the boys.

"He had an obsession with the boys and the Thatcher name," Collver commented.

Dick agreed, and met with JoAnn over dinner. By this time, she had already started dating her future husband, Tony Wilson. Collver and JoAnn talked for a while and reached an agreement. She then asked Tony to come over and speak to Dick. Wilson arrived a few minutes later and the deal was struck.

"The upshot of the meeting was a settlement for $230,000. She wanted custody of the little girl and she agreed that Colin would get both boys," Collver remembers. "I was ecstatic. I thought the matter was settled," he said.

He rushed to phone Colin and told him it was a great deal and that he should take it. Colin's response chilled Dick. "The bitch isn't going to get anything," Thatcher replied coldly.

Collver was annoyed. He told Colin in no uncertain terms that he wasn't going to get involved in his personal affairs ever again. And he didn't. Although he saw Colin later that year, the subject of JoAnn never came up. But the events of Christmas 1979 and the spring of 1980 were to come back to haunt Thatcher at a most inopportune time.

Meanwhile, JoAnn continued her nomadic existence, camping out with a series of friends. In January 1980 she moved into a house in Regina because the owners were going to be away for several months. She was still living off her stocks and bonds from the marriage; Colin hadn't yet paid her a cent in support. He had, however, given her the use of the Thunderbird car they owned jointly. At the end of March, JoAnn's friends returned and she again had to find temporary accommodation in Regina.

The weekend visits were an ongoing problem. Colin had been ordered to stay away from the house so that JoAnn could have time to exercise her parental authority in peace, but he never stuck to the agreement. He'd turn up unannounced and start terrible fights with JoAnn in front of the children.

One of the scenes indicates just how petty he could be. It was Sunday, March 24, and JoAnn was in charge of the Redland Avenue home. She had invited some friends over for dinner. The house was technically hers, after all, since it was still in her name.

She had taken four steaks out of the freezer to thaw for supper. Colin had his steaks specially prepared at the butcher's. They were usually huge T-bones, two inches thick and about a foot across. He liked them cooked to a crisp.

The afternoon had passed peacefully. Greg had invited John Graham, Ron's son, over for a visit. The boys had remained friends despite the obvious differences between their parents.

About 4 p.m. Colin walked into the kitchen unannounced. He spied the four steaks on the counter and demanded to know what was going on. JoAnn told him she was expecting company for dinner. He became outraged and, cursing her, threw the steaks outside into the snow.

Greg was in the kitchen watching the scene. After

Thatcher had thrown the steaks out he returned to the kitchen and told his oldest son: ''This is why Regan refers to your mother as a hooker.''

Colin then started in on JoAnn about her affair with Ron. Referring to the fact that the Graham boy had been over in the afternoon, he told her: ''You can't stay in the same room as John Graham after having run off with his father.''

JoAnn was upset and hurt by the scene. She didn't believe in involving the children in the differences between herself and Colin. She told the court later: ''I have never used foul language in the presence of my children and I have attempted to completely avoid a discussion with any of my children of the difficulties that exist between Colin and myself. I was appalled at the events described and I am greatly concerned about the apparent discussions that my children are being drawn into with respect to the matrimonial differences between myself and Colin.''

The next weekend, Colin told her that if she continued to push for custody of Stephanie and Regan and won, he would cut them both out of his will and leave the entire estate to Greg. It was just another weapon in his arsenal for psychologically harassing JoAnn.

JoAnn was getting fed up. She wanted to get on with her life. She had begun seeing Tony Wilson and genuinely liked the man. She hoped with time that they could build a solid relationship. In the meantime, she was tired of living off her friends' goodwill. She made a motion before the court to get complete control of the Redland Avenue home, and won. Thatcher appealed the decision, but his appeal was dismissed.

The custody battle was still moving forward. The Saskatchewan Court of Appeal heard Thatcher's application to get custody of Stephanie and Regan in early April and dismissed his motion. After consulting with Tony Merchant, however, Thatcher decided to continue his efforts, and instructed Merchant to appeal to the Supreme Court of Canada.

By now, completely consumed with hatred for JoAnn, Colin decided to step up his program of harassment and issued new orders to his household. JoAnn was no longer allowed to stay overnight at the house on weekends, and under no circumstances was she allowed to take the children out. Those orders led to an incident that was to cause JoAnn grief for the rest of her life.

CHAPTER FIVE

Mother Against Son

At about 9:30 a.m. on Saturday, April 26, 1980, JoAnn Thatcher wheeled her car into the driveway of the Redland Avenue home for her regular weekend visit with her children. Technically, she was supposed to have custody of them, but Colin had never accepted the ruling; instead he was taking the custody battle to the highest court in the land.

JoAnn stood outside for a second and looked at the house. She had every right to be there. The access arrangement had been working since October, although there had been some rough spots. What she didn't know that morning was that Colin had changed the rules on her. This weekend was going to be different from the others.

The new rules were part of Colin's master plan to turn the children against her — his way of paying JoAnn, "the bitch", back. He and the boys regularly discussed the ongoing court battles and he encouraged the boys to think in "us-against-them" terms about their mother's attempts to gain custody. He always talked about what "we" were doing against "her".

Colin didn't have the same luck with Stephanie, however. Of the three, she is the only one who has remained consistently affectionate towards JoAnn. She is much like her mother: slim, blonde, artistic and with an underlying determination.

What was about to happen at the house that morning was to demonstrate to JoAnn how far Colin was prepared to go to hurt her, and how powerfully he could twist the young minds of their children to his point of view.

JoAnn couldn't tell if Colin was home because, as usual, there were several vehicles parked in the driveway. She fervently hoped he was away, since his presence guaranteed yet another long, emotional, hurtful scene.

JoAnn had to steel herself for some of the visits. The fights left her emotionally drained from the bitterness and anger. It was tiring, too, not knowing what to expect when she walked in the front door.

For the moment, happily unaware of the new orders, JoAnn planned to take Stephanie to a friend's home that morning. The friend had a small child that Stephanie could play with while JoAnn had a visit. She squared her shoulders and walked to the door. She had the weight of the law behind her and was sure that it was only a matter of time before the Supreme Court of Canada settled the matter once and for all.

She let herself in the front door. Stephanie and Regan were sitting cross-legged, in their pyjamas, watching Saturday morning cartoons in the den.

JoAnn called out a good morning to the children and walked into the kitchen where eighteen-year-old Sandra Hammond was making breakfast. Greg and Colin were not in sight.

JoAnn and Sandra eyed each other warily over the kitchen table. Neither liked the other very much, and the tension in the kitchen was palpable. Since JoAnn had left, Sandra had become a very important person in the Thatcher household. Because of Colin's frequent absences, she ran the home, in her efficient way, and her word was the last word.

As Sandra put the children's breakfast on the table, she informed JoAnn that she wasn't to take Stephanie

51

anywhere. The children came bounding into the kitchen then, so JoAnn ignored Sandra and sat at the table beside Stephanie. She helped the child with her breakfast as she told her they were going to visit a friend whose child Stephanie could play with.

While JoAnn was occupied, Sandra slipped out of the kitchen and up the stairs to wake Greg. She went into his bedroom and shook the sleeping teenager. Greg listened to what Sandra told him, climbed out of bed, pulled his trousers on and walked into the hall.

The sleepy-eyed, tousle-haired boy met his mother coming upstairs to get clothes for Stephanie. He told her that she couldn't take the little girl out until Colin came home, but JoAnn went on by and continued down the hall to get Stephanie's clothes.

Back in the kitchen, with Sandra and Greg watching in silence, JoAnn dressed the little girl. She asked Stephanie to come with her, and the child thrust her arms up. JoAnn picked her up and turned to leave the kitchen.

At that point, all hell broke loose. Both Sandra and Greg started yelling at JoAnn, telling her Colin had said she wasn't allowed to leave the house with Stephanie. JoAnn replied that she had every right in the world; she had a court order spelling out her rights.

As JoAnn turned to leave, with Stephanie in her arms, Sandra leaned forward and grasped JoAnn's wrist in an attempt to stop her. JoAnn shook the girl's hand off and walked to the back door. That was when Greg leaped into action. Bigger and stronger than his mother, he was also unencumbered by a small child. He stood in front of the back door, blocking JoAnn's way, and yelled at her to put the child down and do what she was told. With Stephanie still in her arms, JoAnn wheeled and ran, in her high-heeled, thin-strapped shoes, to the front door. But Greg pushed past her and blocked her way again. She turned and ran back to the back door. There, her son tried to wrench the child from her arms. The pair pushed and pulled for a second before JoAnn, fearing the little girl would be hurt, relinquished her hold on her daughter.

At that point JoAnn tried to assert herself and establish her authority. She informed Greg that she was allowed to do this and intended to take the child, then again tried to pick Stephanie up. As JoAnn approached, the pair started to scuffle and she stepped on his bare foot.

Howling with pain and shouting indignantly that JoAnn had deliberately tried to break his toes, Greg came after her and gave her a shove. A petite woman, JoAnn lost her balance and fell backwards. She smashed the side of her face on a wooden rocking chair, knocking it over as she tumbled to the floor. Her sunglasses flew off the crown of her head and ricocheted into a corner.

Greg was seething with violence and shouting at her as he continued to push her. He thrust at her with the anger of a little boy and the strength of a young man, knocking her down again as she attempted to rise. She flew back and landed on the floor of a closet, smashing her head as she did so. She looked up with growing horror at her first-born.

"You fucking woman," JoAnn recalled him shouting at her.

To JoAnn he looked remarkably like Colin in one of his rages. The violent temper and the desire to be in control were there. He towered over his smaller and weaker mother as she lay helplessly on the floor. Gradually, the realization of how powerful Colin's influence was dawned on her. Colin had broken the bonds between mother and son.

Regan turned in his chair to watch. He coolly witnessed the tableau and left the table without a word. He walked from the room without ever raising a finger or saying a word to help his mom. Sandra was silent, too. Who knows whether she felt any sympathy for the woman she constantly called "the bitch"?

Stephanie ran from the kitchen into the garage and stood crying by her mother's car, repeating over and over that she wanted to go with her mommy, whereupon JoAnn shouted to her from inside the house to get into the car, that she'd be there in a minute and they'd leave. She tried again, desperately, to get past Greg, who now blocked the way into the garage. Suddenly, he turned and ran towards the car, grabbing Stephanie as he did so.

JoAnn was right on his heels. The pair struggled over the little girl, who cried as her mother and brother fought over her.

JoAnn was angry now. She scratched Greg as she desperately tried to claw Stephanie from his grasp. At one point her mouth and teeth came in contact with his arm and she may have bitten him. Because of his superior size and strength, however, the final outcome was never in doubt. With a final shove at his mother, Greg turned and pulled Stephanie through the garage door, into the house. He slammed the door shut and locked it. When JoAnn ran out of the garage to the front door, she found she was too late. Someone in the house had beaten her there and locked it, too.

Totally frustrated, JoAnn walked back to the garage door and hammered on it, screaming to Greg and Sandra that she'd be back to claim her children. Then, finally exhausted, she gave up and slipped into the driver's seat of her car. When she examined her face in the rear-view mirror, she saw that already there was a considerable bruise, which had started to swell.

JoAnn backed the car out of the garage and onto the

street, drove to a pay telephone and called her lawyer and friend, Gerry Gerrand.

Gerrand didn't mind receiving an early morning call on a Saturday from JoAnn, despite the fact that her divorce case was taking more and more of his time. He liked the woman and believed she should have custody of the children. He listened gravely as she spilled out the sordid story, then advised her that there was nothing he could do at the moment and she should let the matter go for the time being.

Gerrand knew there would only be another scene if JoAnn went back to the house that day. If Colin was there when she arrived, the scene could be worse. If she waited, Gerrand would bring the incident up when the matter came to court.

Inside the Thatcher house, more phone calls were being made. Gregory tried unsuccessfully to reach his father. He then tried his father's divorce lawyer. When he, too, proved unavailable, Greg phoned Tony Merchant in Regina.

Merchant listened to Greg's story. Greg said that JoAnn had deliberately tried to break his toes while he attempted to prevent her from taking Stephanie out. He had, he said, only wanted JoAnn to wait until Colin came home before she took Stephanie anywhere, upon which JoAnn had exploded into violence.

He said that his mother had cursed at him, screamed at him and tried several times to crush his feet. Angrily, he reported that she had scratched his back and drawn blood and had also tried to bite him.

Merchant listened to the story and gave Greg basically the same advice Gerrand had given JoAnn. Nothing could be done that day, but the matter would come up during the divorce trial and the custody battle. Greg then hung up to wait for Colin's return.

When JoAnn had finished her phone call, she drove

back to the home of the friend with whom she was staying until she could gain possession of the Redland Avenue house. She must have felt anger at Greg, at that moment, but also shock at how deeply entrenched in him Colin's attitudes were.

JoAnn had never really seriously attempted to get custody of Greg. Even when she had fled from Colin the summer before, she had taken only the two youngest children. But she had clung to the hope that Greg might join them at some time and that she could establish a loving mother-son relationship with him in the future.

Colin's love letters, written to her in August, had mentioned Greg's sadness at their break-up and the boy's hope that the couple would reconcile. And when she had returned from Brampton in the fall, Greg had greeted her warmly and indicated that he was prepared to continue their relationship.

Gradually, however, her hopes had ebbed, as Greg refused to spend time with her and the two youngest children. She knew it was futile to push him and hoped that time would heal the wounds.

But the fight that morning was to drive all those hopes from her mind. Gregory's personality was beginning to be like Colin's. All she could do was try to prevent the same fate befalling her second son, Regan. She vowed to continue the custody fight for Regan until the bitter end.

Both JoAnn and Greg filed sworn affidavits about that morning's incident, which was to become a pivotal event in the renewed battle for custody of Regan later that summer.

On May 5, 1980, the Supreme Court of Canada turned down Colin's bid for custody of the two youngest children. And on May 8, 1980, JoAnn took possession of the Redland Avenue home. Although she finally had a home base, JoAnn's troubles were far from over;

twice while she was away from the house it was broken into, but that was a minor headache compared to her problems with Regan.

On May 14, Regan was finally delivered into JoAnn's care by Colin. Thatcher said the boy was heartbroken at having to live with JoAnn. In court, he asserted that he had taken Regan out to the ranch to explain how it was supposed to be from now on. However, Stephanie reported to her mother that she had heard Colin tell Regan that if the boy kept running away from his mother, eventually the court would have no alternative but to let him live with Colin.

Within minutes of arriving at his mother's home, Regan was gone. He ran out of the side door and hopped on his bicycle. JoAnn drove over to pick him up. In the confrontation with her husband that followed, Thatcher shouted at JoAnn in front of the young boy: "When are you going to leave this poor kid alone?"

That day, JoAnn made a tough decision. "I had come to the conclusion that I could not continue to live in the city of Moose Jaw with the children and retain my physical and emotional health," she told the court. She decided to move to Regina. In the meantime, she planned to visit friends in Roulcau, Saskatchewan, taking the children with her.

The next day, when JoAnn went to pick Regan up at school for the lunch break, he wasn't there. Immediately she phoned Colin. He denied even seeing the boy that day. "If you were any kind of a mother your son would stay home," he said spitefully.

JoAnn left Stephanie with a friend and spent the lunch hour searching for Regan. She found him after school and drove both children home. When Regan found out that JoAnn was planning to take them to Rouleau, he darted for the door. She followed and, as he started to open it, she pushed it shut. But his arm was in the door. At that point Stephanie started to cry. When JoAnn turned to her, Regan shot out the door and was gone.

Again JoAnn hunted for her son. At 8:30 p.m. Colin called and said the boy was with him and wanted to stay the night. JoAnn called the Moose Jaw police, who had to physically pick up the boy and bring him home.

JoAnn took Regan to Rouleau, and the three of them stayed there until May 19. She made arrangements to stay with friends in Regina until she could find a permanent place to live.

It took yet another court fight to get her possessions out of the Redland Avenue house. Eventually, armed with the judge's list of the contents she was allowed to take, and backed by a police escort, she retrieved her belongings.

JoAnn's continuing troubles with Regan were at the root of her decision to move to Regina. The week she spent at the Redland Avenue house was disrupted by constant disobedience from Regan and interference from Colin.

But Regan ran away again in his first recess at his new school in Regina. He hitchhiked to Moose Jaw and rejoined his father. JoAnn saw him for only an hour after that, until the custody decision in August 1980 by Mr. Justice MacPherson.

During this time, Regan was examined by several psychiatrists and psychologists, who testified at the eleven-day custody hearing. Mr. Justice MacPherson called Regan's tale a ''long and dreadful story of interference, contempt of court and downright deception by Mr. Thatcher.'' The account of the fight between JoAnn and Greg was, he said, the most ''distressing'' evidence of the trial. He didn't believe Greg's version of the events and said so.

His considered opinion of the episode constituted a powerful indictment of Colin Thatcher's personality:

> Gregory's belligerence was apparent when he testified that his mother started the whole thing by trying to break his toes by stomping on his bare feet. He recounted indignantly, as if it was a schoolyard fight, how she had scratched him so seriously she drew blood, and that she bit him.
>
> He is a tall, handsome and intelligent boy. He testified for well over a half day. He said nothing at all critical about his father. He rejects the mere suggestion of wrongdoing on his father's part. In many ways he reflected his father's personality — arrogant, proud, vain, even belligerent. For his mother he showed only scorn, contempt and disrespect. His professed love for her was, I felt, insincere. He had no regret for the force he had used upon her. He was simply obeying his father's orders, which was his justification.
>
> Most tragic in Gregory was his complete lack of any consideration for his mother and even for her friends. One is entitled to wonder whether he has consideration for anyone. My marginal note to myself during this testimony was that he was hard, cold and callous.
>
> The violence may have started when Mrs. Thatcher, to get Gregory out of the way [she was still holding Stephanie in her arms], stepped on Gregory's bare toes. I cannot believe that this woman intended to hurt her son.

The judge concluded that JoAnn was a kind, loving woman, a better parent than Colin, and that she deserved a chance to save Regan from becoming a mirror image of Colin and Greg.

One of the reasons given by Mrs. Thatcher for not taking Gregory when she left home last summer was that Gregory had become very close to and very much like her husband. Her principal reason now for wanting custody of Regan is that the same fate should not befall him. Before she made that comment, I had already begun to wonder whether if I committed Regan to the custody of his father he would become another Gregory in a few years.

It was strong and unusual wording, but the judge was saying what he felt had to be said. Well-liked and respected in legal circles, he has a reputation for using strong and colourful language when he feels the need.

The judge didn't condemn Greg entirely for the events. He put the blame squarely on Colin's shoulders, pointing out that Colin had never disciplined Greg for beating up his mother: "Mr. Thatcher did not consider that the acts of Gregory on these occasions deserved any discipline or admonishment. Gregory must have known that his father approved."

The judge added, "I know Mr. Thatcher much better now. His methods and purposes have been to destroy his wife in the minds of their children. In so doing, he has gone a long way towards destroying the children themselves."

Mr. Justice MacPherson lambasted Colin for poisoning the minds of Greg and Regan against JoAnn, and said in open court that Colin was diabolical, foolish and contemptuous. "I must comment that one expects from a member of the Legislature a greater respect for the law than has been demonstrated by him throughout this conflict. One would expect a father, particularly one of such eminence, to show by example to his sons that the law is to be obeyed and the truth told."

The judge had words of praise for JoAnn. He pointed

out that she was enduring a public scandal because she believed she had an obligation to help her son Regan. JoAnn had the capacity for love and understanding where Colin did not. She was able and willing to teach the children the moral values of truthfulness and the difference between right and wrong. ''I feel that she is able to provide the emotional needs to Regan's personality and character which the father's egotism and materialism will not provide.''

A psychiatrist testified at the trial that JoAnn was ''mature, strong, of superior intelligence and education,'' adding that she was a warm person and well-qualified to be a good homemaker and mother.

The judge eventually decided that the best place for Regan was with JoAnn without any influence or interference from Colin or Greg. ''I possess a consuming fear that Regan will develop into an unsympathetic and inconsiderate, domineering adult like his father if I award his custody to his father. . . . If the child is to be saved from becoming the image of his father, only his mother can do it. She wants to try. She has had no chance. That has been denied her for nearly a year by the actions of her husband and Gregory. She will have a difficult time of it, probably extremely so. But Regan is her son and an intelligent boy.''

The judge ordered the boy into his mother's custody and decreed that Colin or Greg couldn't talk to him for a year. In addition, he ordered Colin to pay all of JoAnn's legal costs, despite the fact that he felt costs were sometimes used as a ''licence to plunder''.

The costs must have been welcome news to Gerry Gerrand. He had devoted almost all of his time to the case for the past several months. The property settlement had not yet been determined and JoAnn's only source of income was still her stocks and bonds.

JoAnn was elated at the August 1980 decision. Here was the clear-cut ruling she had been waiting for. Now she could take her children and map out a new life for them in Regina, miles from Colin's influence. Even Colin couldn't ignore the strength of the judge's words, she thought; he would be compelled to obey them because of his stature as a politician.

But JoAnn didn't know what was in store for her. Maybe she underestimated Colin's determination and drive to have his own way.

The battle over Regan was really just heating up. It would become increasingly bitter in the months that followed, as Colin proved he believed he was above the law.

Less than a year later, the fight over the boy culminated in the first attempt on JoAnn's life.

JoAnn Geiger at graduation.

A 1960s photograph of Colin Thatcher (*left*) and his parents
Peggy and Ross Thatcher.

The 1962 wedding in Ames, Iowa, of Colin and JoAnn.

JoAnn in happier days, before 1975.

Colin speaking at a nomination meeting
in 1978.

Colin attending a party in Regina after the 1980 opening of the Legislature.

Colin and his sons Greg *(right)* and Regan celebrating victory on election night, 1982.

Colin leaves court after abduction charges relating to his daughter Stephanie were dropped.

Regina lawyer and Thatcher supporter
Tony Merchant.

JoAnn during a 1981 trip to Japan.

The garage of the Wilson home in Regina where JoAnn was brutally murdered.

The abandoned farm where police recorded a conversation between Thatcher and Gary Anderson that was to play an important role in the trial.

CHAPTER SIX

Shopping for a Killer

The fall of 1980 was a very busy time for Colin Thatcher. In addition to his political duties, he had a ranch and farm to operate. He also managed to find time to start a new romantic relationship, kidnap his son, find out about the marriage property agreement and try to hire someone to kill JoAnn.

JoAnn's father, Harlan Geiger, had come up from Iowa to help her get custody of Regan. The pair spent several frustrating days running from place to place looking for him, but their efforts were in vain. JoAnn didn't see her son again for more than a year.

Deciding he had no option but to send Regan away, Colin arranged for the boy to go to private school in Palm Springs and to live with Thatcher's mother, Peggy, at her condominium. Thatcher not only broke the law, but engaged his mother to assist him. Thatcher went to Palm Springs off and on all winter, and so saw Regan frequently. Meanwhile, JoAnn launched a court battle against Colin — this time to force him to obey the custody order. The pair were in and out of court throughout the fall and winter of 1980–81.

When Colin went shopping for a paid killer, he didn't look very far. He approached a man named Gary Anderson who had grown up in the Caron area where Thatcher had his ranch. Anderson is a big, unkempt man with a reputation around Caron as a somewhat dubious character. He's over six feet tall and burly, with brown eyes, thinning brown hair and a scraggly beard. A reformed alcoholic, he is reputed to have a violent temper. He has been convicted of several crimes — among them assault causing bodily harm, pointing a firearm, another assault charge and impaired driving — and has spent time in jail for some of them.

Anderson's criminal history was probably what caused Thatcher to seek him out. Thatcher knew Gary slightly. Thatcher's property adjoined land belonging to Gary's mother, Kate, and Gary had asked Thatcher for permission to hunt on his lands about three years earlier.

In the fall of 1980, Anderson was living in Lethbridge, Alberta. Kate contacted him and told him that Mr. Thatcher, the politician, was looking for him. About a month later, Anderson returned to the Caron area, contacted Thatcher and set up a meeting at an abandoned farm property.

The farm was to become the setting for many of the illegal dealings Thatcher had with Anderson over the next few years. It's a desolate place with a weathered old barn and a red Quonset hut.

Anderson had no idea that fall morning what the influential millionaire wanted to talk to him about and was probably quite shocked when Colin outlined what he wanted Anderson to do. "He asked me if I would be interested in killing his wife. . . . and made me an offer if I would," Anderson later said.

The offer was for $50,000. The first $10,000 was to be paid immediately, the second $10,000 on completion of the job. The remaining $30,000 was to be spread over the next three years.

Anderson turned down the job, for two reasons. First, he didn't believe in killing; second, he didn't like the payment plan that Colin had outlined.

Anderson told Thatcher he would try to think of someone who might be interested in doing the job and would let Thatcher know. The pair parted company. But Thatcher continued to try to recruit Anderson. Every time Anderson was in town that fall to see his family, Thatcher asked him if he'd changed his mind.

Thatcher may have fancied himself a high roller with a lot of street smarts, but $50,000 was a great deal of money, and Gary Anderson was no professional.

By November, Anderson thought he had someone who might be prepared to do the job. That man was Charlie Wilde. The pair had met at the Regina Correctional Centre earlier that year, when Anderson was doing time on an assault charge. Charlie's own criminal record stretched back to 1968. Charlie was a heroin addict, and nearly all of his sentences were drug-related.

Anderson drove over to Charlie's house in Regina and asked if he'd be willing to participate in the scheme. While Charlie was always willing to make some fast money to feed his habit, he wasn't prepared to kill somebody. He turned Anderson down and told him he couldn't think of anyone who was interested in a job like that. But Gary didn't give up, possibly because he saw an opportunity to make some money from Colin and get in good with a powerful man.

Anderson returned to Charlie's home a few days later, at which point Charlie told him he had someone who was interested. They decided the three of them should meet.

Wilde had come up with a man named William Cody Crutcher. He, like Charlie, had no intention of killing anyone, but saw an opportunity to make some fast money. After all, what could Thatcher do? Tell the police he'd been ripped off?

Anderson immediately went back to Moose Jaw to give Colin the good news. He'd worked out the deal with Charlie. He and Cody wanted $15,000 down, $10,000 on completion of the murder and $25,000 in

73

another year's time. Thatcher agreed and gave Anderson an envelope containing $7,500. Gary then set up a further meeting with Wilde and Crutcher in Regina.

The trio got together at the Fireside Lounge in the Sheraton Hotel. Over drinks, Gary told Crutcher that the person who was to be killed was JoAnn Thatcher, then living with Stephanie in a townhouse on Pasqua Street, north, in Regina. Colin had specifically instructed that nothing was to happen to Stephanie. Anderson emphasized that to the two con men.

Anderson and Crutcher got up casually from the table and walked to the washroom. There, Anderson passed Cody the envelope containing the $7,500. Charlie and Gary left the lounge together and Wilde dropped Anderson off at the bus depot to go home. He then caught up with Cody and they split Thatcher's money.

A few days later, Anderson returned to Regina with another $7,500 — the second half of the down payment. Gary and Charlie met once again in Regina, and Anderson turned over $7,000, retaining $500 to cover his own expenses and time.

At the same time he gave Wilde a set of car keys and a photograph of a woman. Anderson told Wilde they were a picture of JoAnn Thatcher and the keys to her Thunderbird.

Wilde drove over to Crutcher's to split the latest bonanza. Both of them looked at the picture. Then Crutcher burned it. Wilde never saw the car keys again. That was just before Christmas 1980.

Anderson had told the pair that the time to do the murder was during the Christmas break, up until the first week of January. Thatcher intended to be in Palm Springs during that time.

By now, Thatcher had acquired some new worries. The judgment on the marriage property settlement, announced on October 20, ordered Thatcher to pay one of the biggest settlements in Canadian history. As well, the matter of Regan had reared its ugly head again. For one of the frequent court appearances, in a nearly unprecedented move, Mr. Justice MacPherson notified the local press and told reporters that although Regan was missing, Mr. Thatcher did "not appear to be concerned about it."

The judge told the press that the matter obviously required "the widest publicity so the child may be found and delivered to the mother" in accordance with the August 11 order forbidding Thatcher to see Regan until the following July.

As the court hearing into Regan's disappearance wore on, Thatcher continued to refuse to reveal his son's whereabouts. That refusal would later land him in hot water with the legal system.

But for the moment, from Thatcher's point of view, the property settlement was more pressing. Mr. Justice E. N. "Ted" Hughes ruled that a fifty-fifty division of the marriage property would be "fair and equitable."

Colin had argued that JoAnn hadn't contributed 50 per cent of the marriage property and that they owed most of it to the generosity of Ross Thatcher. The accumulated property in the marriage was largely the result of the solid foundation that Ross had laid.

Mr. Justice Hughes said he believed that Colin's father had intended all gifts to be split equally between Colin and JoAnn and that whether Ross had considered the possibility of a marriage break-up had no bearing on his decision. However, Colin claimed that he had had a secret verbal agreement with his father, that, on Ross's death, some of the lands given to Colin were to be transferred to Peggy and, on her death, were then to be turned over to Colin. Those lands were still registered to Ross's estate, and there was nothing in Ross's will to corroborate Colin's claim. However, Colin and Peggy both testified that the secret trust was made in the fall of 1969, and Colin's lawyer argued that the "court must either find the secret trust to exist or find both Colin and Peggy Thatcher to be complete liars."

Mr. Justice Hughes didn't agree and said so. "That is a simplistic argument that cannot withstand close scrutiny. Peggy Thatcher is the respected widow of a former respected premier of this province. That she stands in that light in the eyes of her fellow citizens surely cannot of itself resolve the question of secret trust or no secret trust in the respondent's [Colin's] favour," he wrote.

Hughes valued those lands at $358,530. He couldn't find enough evidence to prove or disprove the existence of the secret trust, and ordered that the value of the land be split equally.

The value of the marriage property was assessed, and what Colin had brought into the marriage was subtracted from the total. Other divisible assets in the marriage were: additional land, valued at $994,012.50, $113,715 and $156,731; the house on Redland Avenue, valued at $85,000; farm machinery worth $81,624; cattle and livestock worth $156,000; household contents worth $10,000; stocks and bonds worth $40,000; cars valued at $35,500; and personal effects worth $12,000. He added that list to the value of Ross Thatcher's land and came up with a total of $2,043,112.50. From that he subtracted any outstanding debts.

The bottom line was that Colin was ordered to pay JoAnn $819,648.90. The deadline for payment was April 1, 1981, after which an interest rate of 11 per cent was to be added to the total.

The judge said he realized Colin was concerned with keeping his farming operation intact. "With that debt he now faces that becomes a difficult task, I'm sure," Hughes said. He ordered Colin to pay the amount by February 1, 1981, or the Registrar of Land Titles would be ordered to sell six properties and the properties remaining in Ross's estate. Once JoAnn received her money, she would then be ordered to transfer the title of the Redland Avenue house to Colin.

The settlement was a crushing blow for Colin. As a rancher, he had a tremendous attachment to his land and didn't want to sell any portion of it to pay back "the bitch". He had made alternate plans with Anderson, of course. Those arrangements probably led to the remark he made to some political friends when a colleague commented on the property settlement. Thatcher replied that he had no intention of paying it.

"Why should I pay it?" he said. "A bullet only costs a dollar." Quite a few eyebrows were raised at the comment but nothing was said. Later some of those people were to make sure the authorities knew about it.

Thatcher's love life took a turn for the better around the beginning of October.

That's when he met Lynne Dally. She had just passed her thirtieth birthday. Dally is a beautiful woman of the California blonde type. She usually has a deep tan, which highlights her large green eyes. A slight woman, she tips the scales at just over 100 pounds. And she dresses very well.

Dally is the daughter of a successful lawyer who left the business and purchased the Sheraton Oasis Hotel in Palm Springs. Her grandfather was a judge. She was accustomed to move in wealthy circles, and most of the men who had shared her life had money. She didn't plan it that way, she says; it just happened.

One October morning in 1981 as Lynne walked through the lobby of her father's hotel, a businessman friend stopped her. He asked if she would be interested in meeting a wheat farmer from Moose Jaw. When she stopped laughing, her friend explained that there was a little more to Thatcher than that. He said that Colin was a politician of some stature and added that he had some money.

Lynne agreed to the date, and she and Colin joined the other couple for dinner. The pair didn't really hit it off at first, but they continued to see each other, occasionally at first, and then with gradually increasing frequency.

By November, Colin felt comfortable enough with her to invite her to the opening of the Legislature. Dally agreed to make the trip and stayed in Regina for about a ten-day visit, during which Colin treated her very well.

Lynne liked Colin and looked forward to seeing him when he returned to Palm Springs for Christmas. At the same time, however, she found the way he talked about his ex-wife very disturbing. Colin told her on their second date how much he hated JoAnn, and it was a theme that recurred constantly throughout the relationship.

"He hated her. He was very, very bitter," she said. "He described the custody suit, the divorce settlement, all the trial procedures he went through. He mentioned many times that he would like to kill her or hire someone to kill her."

At first all of this seemed very remote to Lynne Dally. She had never met JoAnn and was convinced that she was a perfectly horrible, evil woman. It was disconcerting for her when, over the months, people Colin introduced her to said that she reminded them of JoAnn. The two weren't especially alike physically, but there must have been something in Lynne Dally's manner that made people who'd met them both think of JoAnn.

"It was creepy," Lynne said.

Colin liked Lynne very much. She was articulate and bright. In addition, she moved in elite circles and knew her way around the world of money. He must have cared for her to include her in one of the most important nights in politics — the opening of the Legislature.

In the beginning, Colin treated Lynne very well. There were no signs of the famous Thatcher temper or the physical abuse that had contributed to JoAnn's departure.

None, that is, until Christmas of that year — 1980. Colin and Lynne were at the condominium she rented in Palm Springs when they got into a tremendous fight and he slapped her. Without missing a beat, she flew back at him and landed a blow on his neck. She was aiming for his face. It stunned him enough that he didn't hit her again — that time.

That one incident wasn't enough to turn Dally off Thatcher. She admits now the attractions he held were money, glamour and power. "All of that, plus a bit of a challenge," Lynne says today.

It would be an understatement to say that theirs was a stormy relationship. The affair was fuelled by powerful emotions that flared up into terrible scenes. Thatcher's ego was a contributing factor. But Mendell had to take some of the blame. She is very articulate and can be quite cutting when angered. Such a combination was enough to drive Thatcher to distraction during arguments.

The slap at Christmas was just the start of the violent thread in their relationship that was to become more noticeable as the months wore on.

About once a month, Mendell says, Thatcher would fly completely off the handle. "I asked him for months and months and months to please go get his blood sugar and his blood pressure checked," she says, but Thatcher never did.

His drinking didn't help his dramatic mood swings. According to Mendell, he was a very heavy drinker, and she often related his moods to his drinking bouts. She describes him as a classic Jekyll-and-Hyde personality. In his rages he would make completely irrational statements and accusations, calling Lynne every name in the book, including "slut".

Although he struck her often in the later months, she revealed that he never used his fists on her face. He did use his fists on the rest of her body, and would hold her with one hand and slap her with the other, while spewing filthy names at her. At just about two hundred pounds and six feet, he towered over Mendell. She was barely half his weight and had no chance against him in his rages.

But even Thatcher drew the line somewhere. Mendell says that he never struck her in front of the children. The beatings or violence always occurred after they had gone to bed or away from the house. Mendell said she could sometimes see the mood coming on, but once it had started, there was no stopping it.

Thatcher also never hurt his children. Occasionally, he would yell at them or make unreasonable requests, Lynne says, but they would answer "Yes, Dad," "No, Dad," in a placating way.

Mendell labels the attitudes behind such behaviour "Calvinistic". That is, "It's okay to treat your women that way, but you just don't treat your children that way."

Mendell had to learn to deal with Thatcher's big ego, too. She said Thatcher often mentioned that it irked him that his Mercedes wasn't the first Mercedes she had been driven in. "But I'd reply, 'Oh, Colin, you haven't ridden until you've been in a Silver Cloud Rolls-Royce,' " she says with a laugh.

Their fights notwithstanding, Mendell points out that it wasn't all bad — certainly not in the beginning, anyway. There were many tender moments, when Thatcher treated Lynne very well, and the abuse didn't really begin until each was emotionally involved with the other.

"The one thing that would delight me with Colin the most was when I could do something or say something that would make him genuinely laugh," Mendell adds. She enjoyed seeing him relax and enjoy himself. He was such an intense individual, she took pleasure in making him laugh from the heart, not with the phony politician's laugh he had cultivated over the years. "I like to think I brought something to his life," she says.

She did comment that even when she did leave, he went to great lengths to bring her back into his life. He would phone her constantly if she was angry and plead and cajole until she agreed to see him again. "He would beg and beg and beg and beg," she recalls.

" 'You're an incredible asshole,' I would say to him, and he'd respond with 'Does this mean we're not going out for dinner tonight?' Of course, I would break down laughing and go out."

He never believed her when she said she was leaving. "He'd say things like 'Dally, have you ever stopped to consider how lucky you are to have me?' He couldn't imagine anyone thinking he was less than wonderful."

In retrospect, Mendell doesn't know why she stayed with Thatcher for as long as she did. "I'm really not as stupid as this story makes me out to be," Mendell says. And she's not. She, like many other women, JoAnn included, probably got caught on an emotional roller coaster and locked into a pattern that was difficult to break out of.

Even so, when the situation deteriorated from bad to truly horrifying, Mendell was lucky. She got out safely.

CHAPTER SEVEN

An Attempt to Kill

While major changes were taking place in Colin's life, JoAnn was striking out on her own to rebuild hers.

On January 3, 1981, she married Tony Wilson, a steel company executive, and JoAnn and Stephanie moved into the house on Albert Street.

JoAnn had become friendly with Tony during the early months of 1980. Life with Tony turned out to be terrific for her. What particularly delighted JoAnn was the relationship between Tony and Stephanie. Tony had seen a great deal of Stephanie while he was courting JoAnn, and he and the little girl had developed a warm, father-daughter relationship. Wilson's two sons, Alex and William, also took well to Stephanie, and the family enjoyed a happy home life. The Wilsons had no idea of the diabolical way in which Colin planned to shatter their happiness.

Colin returned from Palm Springs in January and immediately got in touch with Gary Anderson to find out what had happened to the $15,000 and ask why JoAnn was still alive. Anderson went to speak to Charlie Wilde.

Wilde told Anderson that something had come up with Crutcher that made doing the job impossible. Anderson told Wilde that that was okay, but that Colin said the job could now be done in February, when he would be in Palm Springs again. Obviously, to reduce suspicion and provide an alibi, Thatcher wanted JoAnn killed while he was away.

Time went by and nothing was done. Anderson phoned Wilde at home and asked him to come to Moose Jaw. Colin was understandably upset about the $15,000 and wanted to meet with Wilde himself. Anderson had set up a meeting for the three of them at the abandoned farm property. The next day Wilde drove to Moose Jaw and picked Gary up at a restaurant. The pair then went on to Caron.

At about 8 p.m., a half-ton truck pulled up and Colin Thatcher stepped out. Right away, Colin asked Wilde about Cody Crutcher, or "Mr. Gold" as Crutcher called himself. Colin was concerned about the money and even more concerned about the car keys and the photograph, since they could link him to Crutcher if Crutcher ever decided to talk. Not surprisingly, Thatcher was nervous about being vulnerable to blackmail.

Colin realized that the money was gone, but kept after Charlie about the keys. Wilde agreed to talk to Crutcher and see if they could be returned.

Colin then asked Wilde if he would kill JoAnn. Wilde refused, but Colin pushed him and offered him $50,000 or $60,000. Unable to resist, Wilde said that he'd think about it. But he did tell Thatcher he lacked the means to commit murder, having no gun or money for transportation.

Colin told Wilde that JoAnn had remarried and was planning on spending the Easter vacation in Iowa with Tony and Stephanie. He suggested to Charlie that that might be a good place to do it. He offered to give Charlie some money to go down and purchase a gun.

Charlie was a little bit greedy. He'd already bilked Thatcher of $15,000, but figured that since he was moving from the Regina area anyway, he might get away with ripping Thatcher off again.

The pair made arrangements to meet the following week. Wilde phoned Thatcher at the Legislative Building and Thatcher told him to be at the front steps at 9 p.m. Arriving for the meeting, Wilde parked his car on the opposite side of Albert Street and walked over into Wascana Park. Thatcher came down the front steps and also walked into the park. The two talked briefly.

Wilde said that Thatcher then returned to the parking lot, got his yellow Corvette and drove around to pick Charlie up. The pair drove down Albert Street, past the Wilson home, to the south end, an area of crescents good for aimless cruising.

As Wilde recalls, ''He gave me an envelope with the money and it was $4,500. Then he asked me if I knew where to get a gun and I told him, yes, I know where I can purchase one in Calgary. And he gave me some American money, all used currency. I think there was $1,400 American, or $1,500 American, and $3,000 Canadian. And he gave me the address of her parents in Ames, Iowa, of JoAnn's parents in Ames, Iowa, and told me when they'd be leaving on their holidays and when they'd be there. They'd be there Easter weekend.''

Although Wilde was given the names of JoAnn's parents and their address in Ames, a few blocks from the university, he did not write them down. Much later, when he testified, he couldn't recall the information exactly.

Perhaps typically, however, Charlie Wilde never made the trip to Ames, Iowa, for the Easter weekend. Instead, he was caught in a Brandon drugstore about three hours after it had closed for business. That shopping excursion ended up costing Wilde thirty months in jail. At the time of his arrest he had $200 in Canadian and $1,400 in American money, which was returned to him two months later in the Stony Mountain Penitentiary where he was serving his sentence.

Wilde has been on two drug rehabilitation programs

to try to kick his habit. He's a bright man and apparently had no intention of killing anyone. In all likelihood, he often gets a chuckle out of having ripped off a man like Colin Thatcher. His criminal record, while lengthy, does not contain a single crime of violence. He has been convicted for possession of drugs, impersonation while trying to get a prescription and breaking and entering — all to feed his drug habit.

As one police officer who worked on the case later said: "Charlie Wilde wouldn't hurt a fly." Wilde was well-liked by everyone connected to the case and he took with him many good wishes for a successful rehabilitation.

After getting out of that car in 1981, Wilde did not see Gary Anderson or Colin Thatcher again until 1984.

Not long after this, Colin found himself in trouble with the justice system.

Regan, of course, had not resurfaced and was still attending private school in Palm Springs. JoAnn was continuing to press hard for details of his whereabouts in order to obtain custody of him.

Throughout the early months of 1981, Thatcher had appeared at a number of examinations aimed at locating Regan. Tony Merchant attended with him and gave him legal advice throughout the proceedings. On February 5, 1981, Mr. Justice Ted Noble ruled that Thatcher was in contempt of court for refusing to answer certain questions about where Regan was.

The judge gave Thatcher until February 20 to answer the questions. Out of a total of 306 questions Thatcher answered "I cannot recall" or "I cannot recall specifics" or "I have no recollection" to sixty-one. In addition, on Merchant's advice, he refused to answer another fifty-six questions. Noble reported that of the questions Thatcher did respond to, twenty-two answers appeared "evasive" and another eighty-five consisted of a simple yes or no.

"All of this leaves the clear impression that Mr. Thatcher was, with the help of his counsel, very carefully avoiding, wherever possible, giving information that could be used by Mrs. Thatcher to locate her son, Regan," the judge concluded later.

Thatcher appealed the contempt ruling, but the Saskatchewan Court of Appeal dismissed the motion and gave Thatcher until March 20 to answer the questions and purge his contempt. When that wasn't done, Thatcher was ordered to appear before Mr. Justice Noble on April 28, 1981. When the day came, Thatcher wasn't even present in court. Tony Merchant had filed a memorandum through the court system but did not appear on Colin's behalf. The judge noted that Merchant was physically in the courtroom but didn't participate.

Mr. Justice Noble had read Merchant's memorandum. A well-respected judge in Saskatchewan, he is, if anything, restrained in the tone and language of his judgments. In view of his reputation, what he had to say about Merchant was surprisingly forthright: "I might add that Mr. Merchant seems to want [to have] his cake and eat it too, because the memorandum sets out a five-page argument as to why his client is not appearing. While he is not about to come here and present his argument in the usual form, he seems to think he can take it in the back door in written form. I find this tactic highly improper and, coming from counsel of Mr. Merchant's experience, an affront to the court. Beyond saying that I have read the memorandum and found the argument and submissions in it without merit, I have no more to say about it."

The judge then went on to comment equally forcefully on Colin Thatcher:

Mr. Thatcher is a very successful businessman. He comes from a family that has contributed greatly to the public life of this province. Indeed, he himself has been and continues to be a member of the Legislative Assembly of this province. By almost any standard, Mr. Thatcher has attained wealth, status and position in the life of Saskatchewan. It is therefore regrettable, in my view, that he finds it necessary to frustrate the custody order which required him to deliver Regan to Mrs. Thatcher. It seems incongruous that a lawmaker is prepared to hold an Order of the Court of Queen's Bench in contempt, even though I recognize that family disputes in general, and custody orders in particular, often bring forth very strong emotional responses which can often cloud the normal reaction and the judgment of a reasonable person. In my view, I cannot ignore who the respondent is. Nor can I ignore his position in society. The public looks to its leaders for guidance by example and action. Simply to have the means to fight an order of the court so vigorously indicates Mr. Thatcher has an advantage many citizens could not claim. So, when he commits a contempt of court order, it holds the law and the court up to ridicule, because many members of the public expect people who have attained his stature in society to obey the law.

Mr. Justice Noble went on to point out, in case anyone in the court had missed it, that he felt Thatcher had done a very serious thing: ''I wish to make it clear that, were it not for Section 28 of the Legislative Assembly Act, I would have sent Mr. Thatcher to a period of incarceration for his contempt. However, Section 28 of the Legislative Assembly Act reads: 'No member may, during the session of the Legislature, be liable to arrest, detention or molestation for any debt or any cause of a civil nature.' Because of that I feel I am unable to impose the sanction of a jail sentence on Mr. Thatcher. I must therefore look to other means of imposing a penalty on him.''

The judge then ordered Thatcher to pay a fine of $6,000 for his contempt of court. In addition, he decreed that Thatcher had to pay all of JoAnn's legal costs.

At this time, according to Gary Anderson, Thatcher had a number of other things on the go. When Anderson told Colin that Charlie Wilde was in jail, he reports, Thatcher asked Anderson to purchase a rifle for him. Anderson was able to secure a fairly powerful rifle — a .303 — from a man named Lloyd in Moose Jaw. Anderson says he then turned the rifle over to Thatcher.

Meanwhile, Thatcher was still appealing the marriage property settlement and hadn't yet paid JoAnn any money. Since the matter was under appeal, he was still in possession of all his lands and hadn't had to sell them.

At the beginning of May 1981, the bitterness between JoAnn and Colin was at its most intense. As Colin was later to say, ''It seemed like every time I talked to JoAnn, an affidavit got dropped in court.''

But JoAnn tells a different story. She had been giving Colin access to their daughter one day a week after being ordered to do so by Mr. Justice MacPherson in December. An affidavit filed by JoAnn outlining the situation shows that Thatcher was trying to influence Stephanie against her mother.

''These visits are upsetting to Stephanie,'' JoAnn wrote. ''On occasion Mr. Thatcher will arrive with one of our sons, or Sandra Hammond, who acts as Mr. Thatcher's housekeeper, and while the other persons are visiting with Stephanie, Mr. Thatcher has on occasion sat in our living room and drunk Scotch. On other

88

occasions Mr. Thatcher has spoken about his Private Member's Bill, which he has presented to the Saskatchewan Legislature for the purpose of permitting children to express their preference as to which parent they will reside with in the event of a marriage break-up.''

JoAnn went on to tell the court that Thatcher was trying to entice Stephanie with material things: ''Mr. Thatcher has spoken to Stephanie during his visitations about meeting with her friends in Moose Jaw, enjoying the swimming pool at the Redland house in Moose Jaw and riding on her pony at the ranch.''

JoAnn didn't want Stephanie, who was seven, riding a pony when she had never taken riding lessons. She said she had ''grave reservations'' about this, and added that she felt Colin was trying to influence Stephanie through the comparison of lifestyles.

''I am continuing to attempt to instil in my daughter Stephanie proper life values, and we do not dwell on any discussion of material things in our home,'' JoAnn continued. ''Colin Thatcher, during his visits, constantly holds up the image of a different lifestyle and there is a continuing subtle attempt on the part of Mr. Thatcher to bribe Stephanie emotionally with discussions of material things that he will provide to Stephanie. This conduct is at complete variance with the values that I am trying to teach my daughter.''

JoAnn really feared that Thatcher was trying to lay the groundwork for custody of Stephanie. ''On several occasions in the past six months Colin Thatcher has addressed words to me to this effect: 'I still expect to pick Stephanie out of the gutter and have custody of her.' ''

JoAnn was very upset when she caught Stephanie calling Colin on the sly. The child was phoning him collect so that JoAnn wouldn't know about it. When JoAnn found out, she told Stephanie that she could phone her dad any time, at JoAnn's expense. The mother said the phone calls stopped once Stephanie learned that she could make them whenever she wanted.

All of these comments were part of an application on JoAnn's part to block any access to Stephanie by Colin. At the time, he was allowed to see his daughter for a few hours on Saturday afternoons. He often took the little girl to his office at the Legislature, directly across the street from the Wilson home.

Regan returned to Moose Jaw at the beginning of May. He saw his mother only twice, and the results were disappointing for JoAnn. ''Regan [avoids] my eyes when I engage him in conversation and he appears cold and distant towards me. I verily believe the actions of Colin Thatcher have seriously impaired my relations with Regan,'' she wrote.

On May 9, 1981, Colin and JoAnn met to discuss the marriage settlement. Colin said they came to an agreement before May 17, the date of the first shooting. But other participants say the settlement didn't happen until later that month.

It was during this period, when tempers were running high on both sides, that Gary Anderson says he turned the rifle over to Colin. Anderson advised Thatcher to practise with the rifle.

Anderson says, further, that Thatcher was still pestering him to kill JoAnn and that he still didn't want any part of it. He knew where JoAnn and Tony lived because, he says, Colin took him to the house several times. ''He had shown me the residence here and had explained to me how easy it would be to get her. He also showed where a person would come in and how a person could leave, or exit, from the house or the place. He had also showed me an approximate location where a person could stand to shoot the rifle,'' Anderson reported.

Anderson still declined the job. Thatcher then asked him to rent a car. Anderson went to Scott Ford in Moose Jaw on May 16 or 17 and rented a Mustang.

He said he agreed with Thatcher to leave the car, with the keys either in the ashtray or under the floor-mat, a few blocks from the Redland Avenue house. ''I was to listen to the news reports and when I had heard on the media or the news that the — that some-thing had happened, I was to pick the car up and return it,'' Anderson stated.

On May 17, 1981, at 10:10 p.m., JoAnn Wilson was shot. Tony was upstairs having a shower. JoAnn was in the kitchen doing the dishes.

As she bent forward to remove the dishes from the dishwasher, there was a loud crack. A bullet shattered the triple-glazed door and smashed into her shoulder.

The force of the impact knocked her down onto the kitchen floor. In the first few seconds of panic she thought the dishwasher had exploded. Wilson heard her scream and raced down into the kitchen. He found her sitting on the floor, bleeding. In the sliding double doors was a jagged hole. Wilson realized when he looked at the doors that his wife had been shot. The police and an ambulance were called and she was rushed to the hospital.

News of the shooting was carried by all the local media. Gary Anderson says he heard the news the next morning and immediately went to Moose Jaw.

He picked up the Mustang and took it to a manually operated car-wash where he cleaned it, particularly the licence plates, which were smeared with mud. He then returned the car to Scott Ford. Anderson says he had no further dealings with Colin for some time after that.

JoAnn was in the hospital until June 4. She needed surgery and a brace to repair the damage to her shoul-der. Both she and Tony had no doubt in their minds that Thatcher was behind the shooting and they were very frightened. They hired bodyguards for her room for part of her stay in the hospital.

Wilson said Thatcher turned up at the Albert Street house about a week later, while JoAnn was still in the hospital, wanting to discuss the property settlement.

"At that time," Wilson stated later, "I told Colin Thatcher that I was satisfied he had somehow arranged for the shooting of JoAnn. He didn't deny the assertion and looked at me without any visible expression and said nothing. . . ."

In the weeks that followed, while Tony and Colin were negotiating the settlement, Wilson mentioned his belief several times. Tony said that Colin never denied responsibility for the shooting.

During the first meeting, Wilson said that Thatcher told him it wouldn't be difficult to arrange a shooting. "He said that he was sure that there were many unemployed Vietnam war veterans in the United States, who had been trained to kill, that could be employed for that purpose."

The scene between the two men that day was very frightening for Tony. Thatcher said there was no way he intended "to be bled financially". He offered to pay a million dollars over twenty years without interest. Wilson replied that the court could order Thatcher to pay $600,000 right away, and that they should start negotiating there.

"Immediately following that statement," Wilson recalls, "Colin Thatcher leaped up from the sofa and walked quickly to the door. Before leaving, he turned around and said to me words to this effect: 'If that is the position of JoAnn, you and JoAnn had better take steps to protect yourselves.' "

Thatcher threatened Tony along the same lines at least once more during the negotiations.

The Wilsons discussed the situation and decided

that the best way to stop Colin's terrorizing tactics was to settle as quickly as possible. They also decided to go to Vancouver for a month after JoAnn's release from the hospital. Tony made arrangements to get the time off work.

Colin has a completely different recollection of this time. He says he visited JoAnn in the hospital alone and that she showed him her injury. The pair then had a discussion about Stephanie's safety. "It was not strained, it was quite cordial," Thatcher recalls.

JoAnn and Tony seriously talked about what they should do about the custody of Regan and concluded that perhaps the battle was a losing one. "JoAnn decided the best thing to do in the circumstances was to give up any attempt to exercise her right to custody of Regan," Wilson said. And that's what they did.

JoAnn held a press conference. With her arm in a rigid steel brace and held out at an awkward ninety-degree angle, the pretty blonde woman read from a prepared statement.

She explained to the television and newspaper journalists why she was going to stop fighting for custody of her youngest son. "The fact that I have personally been terrorized during the last eight months was an ingredient of that decision," she informed the press. "For a period of several weeks — and it's all documented by police reports — my tires were slashed, sugar was put into my gas tank and there were phone calls with nobody at the other end."

JoAnn and Tony weren't the only people in Saskatchewan who thought Colin was responsible for the shooting. The Regina police had their suspicions.

The night of the shooting the police went to the home of Tony Merchant, only a few hundred yards from the Wilson home. Merchant was asleep, but when he heard the news he moved quickly. First he phoned Thatcher in Moose Jaw and advised him not to make any statements to the police until he got there. Merchant then jumped into his car and drove as quickly as possible to the Thatcher house, seventy-two kilometres away.

Merchant saw police cars and roadblocks set up on the highway to Moose Jaw, but he wasn't stopped, even though he was driving at speeds greater than ninety miles an hour.

When he pulled onto Redland Avenue, he saw that the street was lined with police cars keeping the Thatcher home under surveillance. Merchant believed it was only a matter of time before the police came to the door to question Thatcher. The pair sat inside, talking and waiting. But the knock on the door never came.

Thatcher later said he told the Regina police they could "search any part of my property, with or without me."

Politician Dick Collver also became very alarmed when he heard the news of the shooting. Once again he phoned his lawyer, Ron Barclay, and reminded him of his Christmas 1979 conversation with Thatcher. "Mr. Barclay told me in May 1981 that as a result of consultation with his partners I [had] no legal responsibilities whatsoever," Collver said later. Once again, he didn't report the conversation to the police, something he was later to regret deeply.

Among the comments that Thatcher reportedly made during this time was one "jokingly" uttered at a political function, to the effect that he had no need to hire a hit man if somebody was going to do the job for him.

As a result of the shooting, JoAnn and Tony settled the property battle very quickly. The order to pay $819,000 was dropped down to $500,000. The deal called for a deposit of $150,000 immediately and four payments of $87,500 over the next five years. The yearly instalments were set to start in Feburary 1983 and continue through until 1986.

Tony was trying to defuse the violent situation by drastically dropping the amount to be paid and spreading it out over a longer period of time. That way Thatcher wouldn't be forced to sell any land to pay JoAnn what he owed her. There was, however, a clause in the contract providing that if a payment was missed, the entire amount would become due immediately.

There was also a clause stating that if either party died, the next payment would be deferred for twelve months. This clause caused JoAnn and Tony some problems. By signing that contract could she be signing her own death warrant?

"If the clause had said if she had been murdered all the money would have been payable immediately, then maybe she would still be alive," Wilson said about the contract several years later.

But JoAnn wanted to sign. She was tired of the fights; she was tired of the terror. She just wanted to settle it once and for all.

Wilson later described JoAnn as "subject to constant terrorizing by her ex-husband." He also said that "JoAnn was extremely frightened for her life." Nonetheless, the contract was signed and, after a fairly lengthy period of recuperation, JoAnn went back to work at her interior design business.

At last the Wilsons began to cherish the hope that they could live their lives in peace.

CHAPTER EIGHT

The Plot Continues

When JoAnn Wilson gave a press conference about her decision to give up the custody fight for Regan, one person watched particularly attentively.

That person was Lynne Mendell. Although she had never met JoAnn, after almost a year of listening to Colin talk about his ex-wife, Mendell had come to believe that JoAnn was a perfectly horrible woman.

Several weeks after JoAnn was shot, Lynne had returned to Canada with the idea of staying for the summer at Thatcher's Moose Jaw home.

She watched JoAnn on television with keen interest. "That's the first time that she kind of became a real person to me," Mendell says.

She knew about the plans to kill JoAnn as early as 1980, Mendell claims, because Colin talked to her about it often. "When I met him he said he had been seeing someone in Saskatchewan he wanted to hire to kill her. . . . He did not give me any names. He said he was meeting the person at his ranch," she recalls.

She remembers the phone call Thatcher made to her the night of the shooting. "He had heard from Tony Merchant that JoAnn had been shot. He didn't know if she was dead or alive," Mendell says. However, because Thatcher had a fear of being wiretapped or bugged, he said nothing further over the phone. He did describe the events of that night to Mendell later, when he visited her in Palm Springs about three days after JoAnn was shot.

"We went to another condominium that he happened to have a key to and he told me about that night," Mendell recalled. "He had put on a disguise, including a wig, and had a car that had been rented—apparently by someone else, not by him — driven to Regina [and] used a rifle that he had been practising with. He would tell me when he was practising. She was apparently in the dining room and he shot her through the window, but he hadn't gauged the thickness of the glass during his practice sessions so he was not totally accurate and got her in the shoulder, rather than his intended target, which I assume would be the chest."

Thatcher also told Mendell in great detail about how he got away from Regina and back to Moose Jaw safely. "At the time he kind of thought it was funny. He mentioned that the Regina police were better than he thought they were. He started home and there were roadblocks between Regina and Moose Jaw. He said he kind of panicked and drove out into the prairie a long ways, circumventing the roadblocks, and drove back into Moose Jaw. That he parked the car several blocks from his house and that he knew he had lost a lot of time and the only thing that really saved him, quote, unquote, was that the police had not come directly, physically, to his house. Apparently they'd called there, but to see that he was there," Mendell reports.

Thatcher was, she remembers, rather "gleeful" at the scare he had put into Tony and JoAnn. "He came back saying, 'Well, I'm in a position of strength now because they know I'm not playing around. They're scared.'"

In Mendell's opinion, Thatcher's hostility considerably abated after that. "He had settled some of the financial arrangements, basically to his satisfaction, and was seeing Stephanie. It was easier. I mean, he didn't talk as much, with as much hostility."

However, Thatcher denied that any of this happened. As he tells it, when he spoke to Mendell the night of JoAnn's shooting, she immediately asked if JoAnn was still alive.

"I said, 'Yes, she's alive,' and she said, 'Oh, shit,' " Thatcher related.

Mendell says that the shooting that wounded JoAnn had a "surreal" quality to it, for her. "It's a little difficult to believe sometimes that things like this actually happen," she explains. "There's still an air of unreality. I didn't know JoAnn. I'd never met her. I had heard up until, you know, not too long ago, only Colin's side of their relationship, and when she was shot it was a strange feeling, but she wasn't killed. And it just didn't really sink in."

Thatcher and Mendell's relationship was a very unstable one. Colin claims Mendell was constantly asking him to marry her, and that he used his marriage problems as an excuse not to.

That's not the way Mendell tells it. She claims that Thatcher had some very tender moments with her and constantly told her he loved her and wanted to marry her. Otherwise, she points out, why would she have stuck around for two years?

However, when she arrived in Canada that summer, she said she had one of the worst experiences of her life.

She had missed her period and started to put on weight—which was readily noticeable, given her tiny frame. She informed Colin, who told her not to worry about it. She said he didn't seem too concerned.

But Lynne was concerned. She took a home-pregnancy test and had trouble reading it. She became convinced that she was pregnant and insisted on talking to Thatcher about it. His indifferent attitude at first upset her, and then angered her very much. However, when she did go to a doctor, she found out that she wasn't pregnant. "I was so mad I told him he'd never know if I'd done anything about it or not," she said. Yet the relationship continued.

Thatcher says he was never in love with her, although there were times when he cared for her very much. He cared enough to have her living in the Moose Jaw home for most of the summer of 1981.

The fact that Lynne didn't get along with Sandra Hammond, however, eventually created friction in the Thatcher household, and that, combined with the ups and downs in her relationship with Colin, finally decided her to pack her bags and head back to Palm Springs.

It was a difficult fall for Lynne. The recession was hurting her father's hotel business. Colin sent Lynne some money to help her out and, later that fall, she rented an apartment and moved into it.

Meanwhile, JoAnn and Tony entered some of the happiest times of their marriage. Both were determined people who had worked hard not to let Colin's bullying get to them. Now they were free of harassment and believed that the troubles with Colin were for the most part over, since everything now appeared to have been settled.

The Wilsons lived a quiet life. They enjoyed playing bridge with close friends, going to the symphony, discussing their jointly owned business and making travel plans. The family meshed well together. Stephanie and Tony's two sons from his first marriage got along well. For the first time, JoAnn was able to live a life free of the tyranny of a husband's bad temper and without fear of violence.

The fall and the Christmas season passed uneventfully. Then, in January 1982, Colin went down to Palm Springs again and purchased a gun. He claims that acquisition of the firearm was triggered by the receipt of seven red roses, which were sent to his condominium.

Lynne was there when the roses arrived (their relationship was now ''on'' again). When Colin walked through the door Lynne commented that one of his girlfriends must have sent the flowers.

A few minutes later, the phone rang. The caller was male and told Thatcher he had better watch out. ''Just calling to let you know, whether you're in Saskatchewan or California, we can get at you any time.''

''I asked him who it was and he just laughed and hung up,'' Thatcher recalled.

As a result, Thatcher took the ''macho'' step of buying a gun.

''I was overreacting to the roses by buying a gun. At the same time I was conjuring up all kinds of images of having to use that gun,'' Thatcher said later.

When he sought out Ron Williams, at the Frontier Gun Shop in Palm Springs that January, Thatcher put himself in the hands of an expert. Williams is a very large, burly man who really knows his stuff. A former peace officer for the State of California, he is now a security consultant in Palm Springs. He owns about twelve handguns himself and uses them to shoot competitively. He figures he has probably reloaded or supervised the reloading of close to a million rounds of ammunition in his life.

Thatcher went to the gun shop several times and engaged Williams in conversation about weapons. On January 29, Thatcher bought a security-six, .357 magnum handgun, made by the Sturm Ruger Firearms Company in the United States. It cost him about $247, in U.S. funds.

After waiting the regulation fifteen days for a security check, Thatcher returned to pick up the gun in February, purchasing a supply of ammunition at the same time. He bought a hundred rounds of Winchester Western .38-special, plus-P, silver-tipped, aluminum-jacketed bullets. Williams said he sold Thatcher those particular bullets because they are designed to stop people.

"It's designed, upon entering a medium such as human flesh, to expand and open up, causing greater trauma, greater blood loss," Williams said. The purchase didn't raise Williams's suspicions, since the .357 magnum is a very popular gun among Palm Springs residents who want to protect their property.

The gun is, of course, illegal in Canada without a special permit which is not difficult to come by. In Canada, the plus-P designation signifies that the bullets are reserved for police work.

Thatcher also purchased a holster, made by the Bianchi Leather Company in California and designed for a Smith and Wesson .38 or a .357 magnum handgun with a six-inch barrel. Thatcher says he later wrote his name and California address on the inside of the gun holster.

That spring Lynne's lease expired, and Thatcher allowed her to move her furniture and belongings into the garage of his condominium. It was good timing for him, too. A provincial election had been called and he had to stay in Saskatchewan, though he had originally planned to take Regan and Greg and their friends to Palm Springs for the Easter vacation. Lynne agreed to stay and supervise the boys, even though they didn't always get along together.

The election went very well for Colin. He handily won the Thunder Creek riding, which he had held since 1975. And, even though he had publicly criticized the new premier, Grant Devine, Thatcher was appointed Minister of Energy and Mines.

Thatcher's ministerial status seemed to add to the already considerable aura of self-confidence that a lifetime of wealth and power had given him. Never very far from the spotlight, he was now thrust back into it, where his flamboyance and flair for controversy ensured he would remain. He had already been suspended from the House on two different occasions: once for calling the proceedings a "kangaroo court"; once for calling the Speaker the second-best in history with all others tied for first place.

Thatcher attacked his new job vigorously. He wanted to throw the doors of the province open to private enterprise, and one of his first projects was to try to implement a new oil royalty structure to attract the business of new oil firms. He also wanted to encourage more foreign investment, criticizing the federal Foreign Investment Review Agency as a drag on the economy.

Thatcher had a reputation for being extremely hard on people. (He admitted that he was blunt, but only because he wanted to make his time count.) And there were those who referred to him as "the J. R. Ewing of Saskatchewan" — an appellation perhaps inspired by his habit of hopping into his yellow Corvette and zooming up to the Legislative Building or surveying his farm fields from an air-conditioned vehicle equipped with a mobile phone.

A story circulated that he had fired an NDP-appointed civil servant over that very phone — a story vehemently denied by Thatcher. He did change some political appointments although, actually, he kept more of the previous regime's employees than other ministers did. As a result, he was also criticized for not purging the ministry of NDP-appointed personnel.

Lynne Mendell had returned to Moose Jaw for the summer believing that she and Colin were to be married. Colin had, she says, spent the entire spring wooing her and begging her to come back to him.

Every day a dozen roses would arrive for her at her father's hotel until, finally, she agreed to meet him for lunch.

At lunch, he proposed marriage.

"Can I tell my friends and family we're getting married?" she asked. And he replied that she could.

Mendell quit her job and moved to Moose Jaw. She appeared with Colin at the swearing-in ceremony for the cabinet. Everything seemed rosy, until, a couple of nights later, after the children had gone to bed, Lynne and Colin had a spectacular fight.

Mendell had started to press Colin on when they would be getting married. She had really committed herself by quitting her job and moving up to Moose Jaw, and she wanted to know what plans they could make.

"The next thing I knew I was picking myself off the floor of the den," she recalls. "He kept hitting me. It went on for the next thirty minutes. It was a kind of craziness and he was punching me around and slapping me, all because he had promised me all of those things," she said.

After he finished he went upstairs to bed, leaving Mendell feeling sick and humiliated. "I started to think: How could I face my friends and my parents after this? After telling them I'd be getting married?"

The more she thought about it, the more it upset her; she didn't know how she could face returning to Palm Springs. It's not that her parents liked Colin Thatcher; by this point, in fact, they disliked him immensely. But she didn't want to admit she'd made a terrible mistake.

Upset by the beating, Mendell says she was seized by a kind of temporary insanity. She went to the kitchen, where she knew Colin had a supply of pain-killers — 292s — and swallowed a large number. Then she returned to the den and sat in the dark, waiting for

103

the pills to take effect. But when she started to feel the first symptoms of dizziness she became extremely frightened.

"This was such a mess. I sat there in the reclining chair and I started to get scared. I started thinking: This is ridiculous, my mommy loves me, my daddy loves me, why am I doing this? Colin Thatcher isn't worth it."

Mendell, by now unsteady on her feet, walked upstairs into the master bedroom and shook Thatcher to wake him from an apparently sound and untroubled sleep. Clearly, the recent scene that had so upset her had not caused him much anxiety.

When he heard what she had done, he jumped out of bed and woke Greg up. The pair rushed Mendell to the hospital where she was given syrup of ipecac, which has an emetic effect. As she lay on the table in the emergency room, pale beneath her tan, Mendell says she realized that Colin was primarily worried about the effect her actions might have on his career. "His main concern was that he didn't want it to get into the papers — 'Cabinet minister's girlfriend tries to kill herself,' " Mendell recalls.

Thatcher has a completely different recollection of the incident that set off the suicide attempt. As he remembers it, Mendell had gotten into a bad fight with the boys, and Thatcher had told her that he couldn't take the constant fighting and that she'd have to go back to Palm Springs.

"It was the dumbest thing I've ever done," Mendell says today of her self-destructive action. "I'm sorry I did it."

A few days later, Colin travelled to Los Angeles on government business. Feeling it would have created awkwardness to accompany him, Mendell stayed behind in Moose Jaw. While Colin was still away, Lynne's mother, Ann, called with some disturbing news.

Ann had the keys to Thatcher's condominium, as well as to a number of others in the area. Since she was a year-round resident, many owners trusted her to check their places once a month for break-ins or any other problems.

When Ann Dally had tried to get into Colin's condominium (where, incidentally, all of Lynne's belongings were stored), she found that the key didn't work. As she stood wondering what to do, the next-door neighbour appeared and, rather embarrassed, explained. She — the neighbour — had received a phone call from Colin about a week before. Without informing Lynne or her mother, he had asked the neighbour to change the locks on the doors and send him the new keys. When Lynne confronted him with the story, however, Colin vigorously denied it.

At that point, Lynne packed her things and left Moose Jaw. It was the second summer in a row that the couple had planned to live together and failed to last past mid-July.

Mendell returned to Palm Springs and told her friends and family the wedding was off. Those who suspected that Colin wasn't treating Lynne properly were relieved.

Back in Palm Springs and living with her parents, Mendell contacted a lawyer to help her gain access to her belongings, which were still stored in Thatcher's condominium. In September, Thatcher came down and opened the place up so she could get her things. She removed some things — mainly clothes, books and art — but did not completely clear out her possessions until quite a while later.

Thatcher maintains that his relationship with Lynne wasn't a particularly special one for him. He cared about her, but didn't actually love her, he says. Lynne doesn't agree. Not only did they spend a great deal of time together, but Thatcher treated her as an important person in his life, introducing her to his friends and inviting her to live with him and his family. It was, she maintains, no casual affair, and she still can't explain Colin's insistence that he didn't love her. " 'Why me, then?' I ask myself. There are girls with longer legs and better bodies. Why did he stay if he just wanted somebody to sleep with? If that's all he wanted, I would have known about it a lot sooner."

When Mendell left Moose Jaw that summer, the relationship was truly on the skids. It was only a matter of time before it collapsed completely.

CHAPTER NINE

Stalking

In the fall of 1982, Gary Anderson entered the picture again. He had been away for quite some time, having taken an out-of-town job and moved away.

Anderson was still quite prepared to help Thatcher. Perhaps he liked the proximity to the power and money that Thatcher represented. The pair would not have had contact in the normal course of their lives but, because of the nature of their business, they continued to keep in touch over the next few months.

That fall, Gary and Colin met once more at the abandoned farm, and Gary asked about the shooting attempt on JoAnn. "I asked him, just asked him, I said, 'Well, how the hell could you miss her at that range?' He just didn't know how he could have missed at that range, just didn't know," Anderson said.

Some months earlier, in Palm Springs, Lynne Mendell had watched Thatcher pack his .357 magnum into a box. She knew he had been practising with the gun out in the desert. He'd collect numbers of large Perrier or Scotch bottles, put them in a bag, load them into the car and drive away from the city to practise.

Thatcher carefully wrapped the gun up in newspaper and placed it in a box, packing it tightly so it wouldn't rattle. "It was from a toy that his daughter had gotten one Christmas when she had been down there. It was a box about the size of a shoebox. It was a shower — a toy shower for a doll similar to a Barbie doll. Something like a Barbie doll shower. I recall because I thought it was a little bit funny at the time."

Mendell had watched in silence as Thatcher put the box into his suitcase and closed it. He had returned with it to Canada.

Now Thatcher needed some help with the gun, according to Gary Anderson. Anderson remembers it being a .357 magnum security special. Thatcher wanted a silencer for the gun, and Anderson agreed to do what he could to help him. There was a holster with the gun, but Anderson saw no need to take it. Anderson went to see a man named Dan Doyle, who worked in a welding shop. The pair made about six silencers, the last of which successfully cut the noise of the fired gun by about three-quarters.

To fit the silencer on, the front sight of the gun had to be removed and the barrel end had to be threaded. The two men test-fired the gun a couple of times and Anderson later disposed of the six steel tubes. He threw some behind his mother's property and tossed the rest into the local nuisance grounds.

In October 1982, one of Thatcher's political workers found something odd in a car Thatcher had asked him to drive. Charles Guillaume, Colin's campaign manager, was asked by Thatcher to drive a government car from Moose Jaw to Regina for him. It wasn't an unusual request; Guillaume occasionally did favours for the minister. The following day, Guillaume picked up the car at Thatcher's Redland Avenue house. Someone at the house gave him the keys and off he started for Regina.

He wheeled the car into the Legislature parking lot and decided to give it a cursory check for overlooked personal belongings.

Under the driver's seat, he found a holster for a gun. Guillaume was surprised, but didn't think much of it and merely tossed it into a desk drawer in his office. A month or two later, he remembered the holster and asked Colin, " 'By the way, did you leave something in the car?' And I showed it to him. And his response was 'Oh, really?' and led me to believe it wasn't his." Guillaume tossed the holster back into his desk drawer and forgot about it for some months.

Colin was having a pretty busy fall all the way around. In spite of rumblings from colleagues that he should be spending more time in the House, Colin and Lynne found time for a trip—first-class—to Europe.

Lynne can't remember exactly when they went to Europe that fall. She admits she suffers from something she calls "Palm Springs time frame" which afflicts people who don't work regular hours and spend a great deal of time maintaining their tans. But she definitely remembers the trip. It was one of the most sordid experiences of her life.

When they arrived in London, they checked into a suite at the elegant Savoy Hotel, then went out and had a lovely dinner. Back in the room, which had separate beds, Mendell felt exhausted. Colin had slept off his jet lag, but she was still suffering. "I got into bed and the lights were out and I said, 'Gee, I've got a headache'," she remembers.

Her next recollection was "Wham, kabam" to her head as Colin struck her twice and towered over her bed.

Thatcher started to shout at her. "You bitch! Don't you know the only reason I brought you to Europe was to fuck?" he yelled, as he struck her again and again. In the darkness, Lynne crouched beneath the covers, trying to shield herself from the blows.

"I thought he was going to kill me," she recalls. "Okay, I was scared to death." She was scared enough to allow him to do whatever he wanted.

"I said, 'Fine, go ahead. If it's so important to you then do it.' And you know what the bastard did? He did do it. It was the classic scene. I just lay there and, after a while, I said 'Are you through?' He got off me and went back to his bed and fell asleep. I lay there for a minute and then quietly slipped out of bed and into the bathroom. I ran a hot bath and just soaked in it.''

Then she quietly phoned the hotel's front desk. '' 'This is Mrs. Thatcher,' I told them, because we were travelling under that name. 'I would like to book another suite for tonight.' They didn't argue. They just sent up the keys. I guess they heard a tone of quiet desperation in my voice.''

She stuck out the trip with him, and there were no more scenes. Once again, Colin had displayed what she calls his Jekyll-and-Hyde personality.

''He was not a nice man. He'd be talking and he'd get that hostile tone in his voice out of the clear blue sky. Sometimes I wouldn't even know why,'' Mendell reveals. The pair weren't destined to stay together for much longer.

Mendell returned with Colin to Moose Jaw for a while before going back to Palm Springs, but what was left of the relationship was in tatters, and she was just going through the motions until she could get things sorted away down there.

Colin came down to Palm Springs with the two boys for Christmas. Mendell, who was still staying at the condominium, noticed that the talk of killing JoAnn had started again. Thatcher was due to pay JoAnn $87,500 on February 1, less than two months away.

That Christmas he carefully discussed the arrangements for making phone calls back and forth with Lynne. ''We were always, always in touch by phone at least once a day. Colin started to, again, tell me over the phone that he was very afraid that, you know, these phones were tapped, etcetera. So, obliquely perhaps would be the word, he told me to please be available for telephone calls at certain times — in the early evening and then again later at night — because he'd

110

be calling me, then he'd be going out and coming back, and he wanted to make sure that I was available so he could make phone calls."

Mendell also remembers that Colin "was driving into Regina every night to check things out; to find, you know, find a night that would be opportune."

Mendell started to stay at the phone between 5 p.m. and 7 p.m. in the evening, and then again from 10 p.m. until 11 p.m. These telephone "vigils" continued until January 21, 1983.

Thatcher returned from Palm Springs around January 9. This time, his reception — at least in Saskatchewan political circles — was very unpleasant. He was asked to resign from his cabinet post by Premier Grant Devine, for reasons that were never made public. Devine issued a statement saying that Colin Thatcher had resigned from his Cabinet post because of family and business pressures.

Thatcher has consistently declined to discuss the matter, citing his oath of cabinet secrecy as the reason for his continued silence. One possible reason, according to insider speculation, might have been the ideological differences between Thatcher and Devine with regard to Crown corporations. The provincial PC government was moving to dismantle some of them and shift them into the private sector. Thatcher felt that there was no need to privatize those Crown corporations that were profitable.

Ideological differences notwithstanding, many felt that probably the abrasive cabinet minister had simply stepped out of line once too often. Thatcher had been absent from several cabinet meetings. Moreover, he had also been making arrangements to move the offices of Saskatchewan Oil, of which he was chairman, away from the Legislative Building, because, he claims, he was growing tired of the atmosphere of rumour and gossip that surrounded him there. There was also the matter of his continued practice of giving government business to Tony Merchant's firm — a practice that may have been unpopular with good Conservative lawyers; though, had the Conservatives been in power federally, it's less likely this would have posed a problem for Thatcher. At any rate, for whatever reasons, his resignation took effect on January 17.

When she heard the news of Colin's demotion, JoAnn Wilson immediately became alarmed. Colin had left the Wilsons more or less alone since the shooting, and as long as he was kept busy with his portfolio JoAnn felt relatively safe from his harassment. But she knew how a man of Colin's pride would react to the public humiliation of losing a prestigious post. Add to that the fact that Thatcher felt he had his father's reputation to live up to and JoAnn felt she had real cause for concern. Colin might now feel he had nothing left to lose.

On January 20, Gary Anderson, now working in La Ronge, Saskatchewan, some distance north of Prince Albert, drove from there to Caron to visit his family. On his way to the farm he met Colin driving the tractor, moving feed to some stock he had out in the field. Anderson stopped and asked him how it felt to be unemployed, referring to Thatcher's dismissal from the cabinet. The pair chatted for a few minutes.

"At that time I recall he mentioned to me he was stalking his wife that week. He had stalked her at her garage in Regina. He had told me at that time, he had been down the previous night but didn't get her," Anderson recalled later.

Thatcher asked Anderson if he still had the .357 magnum he had given him the previous fall. Anderson did indeed have it. It was in a dresser drawer at his mother's house. Colin and Gary made arrangements to meet the next day for the transfer of the gun.

Despite the number of vehicles that Colin Thatcher

owned, on January 10 he signed out another car from the Saskatchewan Legislature car pool — a blue 1980 Oldsmobile Delta 88, licence number KDW 292. That car was to figure in some odd events in the vicinity of the Wilson home the week before JoAnn was murdered.

Joan Hasz had kept house for ten years for a family who lived a few doors west of the Wilsons, and knew the neighbourhood well. A few weeks before JoAnn's killing, she began to notice a blue car regularly parked on the street. At first she assumed that the car's driver was simply visiting friends in the neighbourhood, but then, she said, "it seemed that it was always there."

On Wednesday, January 19, something about the car began to make Mrs. Hasz nervous, and she consciously began to keep an eye on it.

"I just got a feeling that it was up to no good. I don't know, I just got that feeling. It got on my nerves and I just felt I had to watch," she said. She first began really to take notice of it at about 3:30 p.m. the afternoon of January 19. It was parked directly across the street from the house where she worked.

As she watched, she saw that a man was sitting in it, slumped down in the driver's seat as if trying to avoid being noticed by passers-by. She watched the car until about 5 p.m. when she started preparing dinner for the Adams family. When she left that evening, the suspicious blue car was gone.

The car reappeared the next day, in almost exactly the same spot, at about 3:45 p.m. Again a man sat behind the wheel of the car. He wore some sort of dark toque and a dark coat, and had a well-trimmed beard.

This time, Hasz also noticed his hands. "He seemed to have some very tight gloves on, those real skintight gloves. Well, they were a kind of a white steelish-blue colour, sort of a light colour, almost like those rubber surgical gloves . . . You could really see the fingers

113

and he seemed to keep doing something down here with his hands that drew my attention to them."

She watched the car until almost 5 p.m., when Duane Adams came home from work. He, too, had noticed the car and its occupant. "The person was curious in the sense that when I drove up to my house, our eyes locked momentarily and then he squirmed out of the way to avoid seeing me, or my seeing him," he recalls. "I noticed that he had something on his hands, which were ghastly white, and I found that curious. And the obvious — there seemed to be some obvious tension. . . . You can sometimes feel something even at a distance. This fellow was nervous, he didn't want people to see him, and he didn't know we were watching him."

The occupant may not have wanted the neighbours to notice him, but Joan Hasz had done even more than that. That Thursday evening, as she got into her own car to go home, she noticed that the blue car was still there.

"I just felt that he had been watching me as much as maybe I had been watching him, and I was afraid; of what, I didn't know — I was afraid of something," she recalls.

She looked at the licence plate of the car and noticed that the first three letters were smeared with mud. She wanted to scrape the mud off to get the full licence number but was afraid that the driver would spot her.

Somebody had once told Mrs. Hasz that a car could be traced using only the last three numbers of the licence. Mrs. Hasz jumped into her car and repeated the number "292" all the way home so that she wouldn't forget it.

The car was seen and noticed by two other people that week. On Wednesday afternoon, RCMP Corporal Donald Forth, a vehicle identification instructor, noticed a car driving on Broad Street in Regina. It struck him as odd that the car, which was relatively clean, had its licence plate obscured by mud. As he pulled alongside the car, he noticed that the driver wore a dark toque and a dark jacket and was either unshaven or lightly bearded. Forth made a mental note of the occurrence.

The following afternoon, just after 5 p.m., Margaret Johannsson left work at the Legislative Building and walked westward on 20th Avenue, on her way home. A short distance from the Wilson house, she noticed the blue car and its lone occupant. Her description of the driver matched those of the other witnesses. She particularly noticed the man because the car wasn't running. She tried to read the licence number after she had passed the vehicle, but couldn't because it was covered in mud. That was the last time anyone noticed the car in the neighbourhood.

The next morning, the day of the murder, was overcast and cold — below freezing. Thatcher and Anderson met in the morning and went for a drive, to the north of Caron, in Anderson's 1974 Mercury — a big, very fast car with a 400-cubic-inch V-8 engine, automatic drive, power steering and brakes and a two-barrel carburetor.

Thatcher asked Anderson if he could borrow his car that evening. They arranged to meet several blocks from Thatcher's home in Moose Jaw at about 1 p.m. that afternoon. Anderson drove down the street, stopping to pick up Thatcher, who was standing in the middle of the road. On the way to the bus depot, Anderson turned the handgun and a bag of ammunition over to Thatcher. Before Anderson got out of the car Thatcher reminded him to listen to the news. If anything happened to JoAnn, Anderson was to return to their present location in Moose Jaw to pick up his car. If there was anything left in the back seat, he was to destroy it. Anderson agreed and left the vehicle.

115

From there he went to the dentist, then to have his hair cut. He was sitting talking to a friend at 6 p.m. on the night of the murder.

When the killer left the Wilson garage that night, he left a very important piece of evidence behind. A credit-card slip was found about four feet from the southeast corner of the garage.

It was a single-folded credit-card slip lying on top of a bank of snow. The slip, dated January 18, 1983, recorded the purchase of $29 worth of gasoline, bought at the J and M Shell Service Station in Caron, Saskatchewan.

The signature on the credit-card slip was Colin Thatcher's.

CHAPTER TEN

The Sting

The news of JoAnn Wilson's murder spread like a prairie fire on a dry August day.

Inspector Ed Swayze, of the Regina City Police, was enjoying a drink with colleagues at one of the local bars. Ironically, they were discussing the first shooting of JoAnn when the phone rang for Swayze. It was his wife, Marion, a bright and vivacious woman. She had heard the news of the murder and wanted to let her husband know.

Swayze is an immensely likable man with a fine sense of humour. He's also as tough as a steel trap and a very good cop. This was his case and he was convinced that Colin Thatcher was the man he wanted. He held that belief tenaciously through the next fifteen months.

The murder sent shock waves through the city. Fearing that Thatcher might be settling old scores, a number of people fled their homes. Among them was a judge who had presided over part of the divorce case. He left his home and checked into a hotel when he heard the news.

The first police car arrived at the Wilson house at 6:05 p.m. Constable Joseph Fraser, a seven-year veteran of the force, was about five blocks away when he got the radio call. It took only a minute for him to get to the Wilson residence.

Fraser pulled his car up in front of the driveway just as another police car arrived. There was no one in sight,

117

but Fraser could see Wilson's body lying in the garage. He knew immediately that she was dead and went back to the cruiser to call for assistance. Fraser remained at his post throughout the ensuing investigation to guard the scene. Calls were going out to various experts. Homicide and identification units were called, as well as the coroner's office.

Constable Thomas Schuck arrived at about 6:10 p.m. The last vestiges of daylight were rapidly disappearing, so Schuck used his flashlight to look around the grounds for clues. After about fifteen minutes, his light focused on a piece of paper lying on the snow about four feet from the corner of the garage.

It was a credit-card slip. Schuck tried unsuccessfully to make out the name, initialled the back of the slip and turned it over to Sergeant Bob Murton. Murton and his partner, Sergeant Jim Street, were the investigating officers on the scene. The slip was completely dry, suggesting that it had lain on the snow for only a short time.

Meanwhile, in Moose Jaw, a police car pulled up in front of the Thatcher home, although no one ever checked to see if Thatcher was indeed there. However, Staff-Sergeant Wally Beaton was later to find telephone company records showing a call from Thatcher's home to Lynne Mendell at that time.

It was a terrifying call for Mendell. Thatcher told her that JoAnn had apparently been shot and killed. Tony Merchant had driven by the Wilson house, seen the police cars and phoned Thatcher.

Back at the murder scene, the identification expert was just arriving. Constable Walter Fryklund, a photographer and fingerprint expert, had received the call about 6:15 p.m. He prepared the equipment he needed, picked up his partner, Corporal Edward Pearson, at his house on south Albert Street, and went to the scene.

When he arrived, at 6:35, Fryklund immediately began to photograph the scene and the body. JoAnn was lying at the back of the Audi, face down on the garage floor, with her head pointing towards the street.

Fryklund took pictures of the untouched garage and measurements of the surrounding area. Then JoAnn's body was rolled over and he took more pictures. Murton and Street instructed Fryklund what photographs to take and Fryklund took a few extras that he believed were necessary. He took somewhere between eighty and a hundred photographs, frequently changing the settings on his flash to ensure he had covered all bases.

By 6:45 p.m., the chief pathologist from the Regina General Hospital had also arrived. Dr. John Vetters got the call at home at about 6:30. He had moved quickly, and now he did some preliminary investigation in the garage, along with the chief coroner, Dr. Stewart McMillan. Vetters left about 7:30 and returned to the hospital to wait for the body.

The police investigation in the neighbourhood continued. When Duane Adams and his wife left their house at about 6:30 on their way out for dinner, they found the area sealed off. When Duane learned what had happened at the Wilson house, he volunteered the information about the man in the car whom he and his housekeeper had observed that week. The police immediately put Adams in the back of a cruiser and asked him to write out what he could remember. He then left for dinner with his wife.

Inside the Wilson house, Craig Dotson was undergoing a similar experience. After interviewing him, the police asked Dotson to accompany them to see a police artist. Dotson was the closest thing they had to an eyewitness. Dotson spent more than an hour with the artist as she painstakingly changed the drawing over and over again to tally with his description. Dotson left that night before the final version was complete and saw it again in the newspaper the next morning. He was not completely satisfied with the sketch, which was scarcely surprising, since he'd had only a fleeting glimpse of the man, in a poor light.

By 7:45 p.m., the initial investigation at the garage was almost complete. JoAnn Wilson's body was loaded into Olson's Ambulance and taken to the hospital. Constable Joe Fraser, the first man on the scene, rode in the ambulance. Although Vetters was waiting at the hospital, he didn't do his autopsy until the following morning.

Dr. Vetters started work the next day about 9 a.m. He was joined by Constable Walter Fryklund, who took photographs throughout the autopsy, and by RCMP Staff-Sergeant Arnold Somers, a firearms expert from the Crime Detection Laboratory.

Vetters established that JoAnn had died from the bullet, not the beating. At least fourteen bullet fragments were removed from her brain. (Some were so small they couldn't be removed.) As Vetters took out the pieces he turned them over, fragment by fragment, to Somers, who was standing nearby.

The pathologist examined the wounds on JoAnn's head and hands closely. From them he was able to discern that the weapon that had caused them was sharp and had some weight to it. Because most of the cuts were very short in length, it was apparent that the blade was also curved. Vetters believed that the killer had probably used a meat cleaver. The bruising, he decided, occurred when JoAnn managed to deflect the cleaver or turn it so that the flat of the blade struck her. Her clothing was drenched in blood and yielded no clues, other than the cause of the bruise on her neck, which probably occurred when the killer wrenched taut the collar of her fur jacket, with its metal clasp, to hold her in place during the beating.

Staff-Sergeant Somers had hoped to discover, from the pattern of any residual gunpowder, clues to the type of gun used. Possibly the flow of blood had washed off any residue; possibly the muzzle of the gun had been too far away from JoAnn for any powder to have been distributed on her; or possibly there was a cloth wrapped around the gun or some paper between the gun muzzle and the target. In any case, no powder residue could be detected.

Outside the hospital autopsy room, the police investigation was moving forward. That day, during another search of the Wilson garage, the police found one of JoAnn's contact lenses on the floor. They also started a door-to-door enquiry in the neighbourhood to see if anyone had noticed anything suspicious around the Wilson home. That was how they located Margaret Johannsson, the civil servant who had seen the blue Oldsmobile outside the Wilson house the day before the murder. They had, of course, already interviewed Joan Hasz, whose name Duane Adams had supplied.

Tony Wilson had sent Stephanie to a neighbour's house to play that day. Thatcher turned up just after noon asking to see her. Wilson, who believed Thatcher had killed JoAnn, slammed the door in Colin's face and shouted that he couldn't see her. Thatcher immediately went over to Tony Merchant's to discuss what he could do. Merchant believed that Thatcher, as the only surviving natural parent, now had a primary right to Stephanie. He thought it was only a matter of time before Thatcher was given legal custody of the little girl.

The pair went over to neighbour Susan Kohli's home, where, they had learned, Stephanie was staying. They let themselves in the front door and called out. Thatcher walked directly in and picked Stephanie up. Susan Kohli, a small woman, threw herself at Thatcher, but only managed to rip one of the belt loops from his pants, as he fled from the house with Stephanie clutched in his arms. Kohli immediately phoned Wilson, then the police.

At 4 p.m. that afternoon, Staff-Sergeant Wally Beaton walked up to Thatcher's Moose Jaw home and knocked on the door. Thatcher and Stephanie were taken to the police station, where they were detained for about two and a half hours. Stephanie was returned to Tony Wilson's care, and Thatcher was charged with abduction and mischief. Tony Merchant faced the same charges. Undaunted, Thatcher immediately launched an application to obtain permanent custody of Stephanie.

By January 23, the police had pieced together the story of the blue Oldsmobile with the 292 licence plate from what Joan Hasz was able to tell them. Sergeant Gene Stusek found the car parked about a block south of 1116 Redland Avenue. Colin turned the keys over to Stusek, who examined the inside of the car and trunk, took a series of colour photographs and left.

By this time, Gary Anderson had read of JoAnn's murder in the Saturday newspaper. He waited until Sunday and got his brother-in-law to drive him to Moose Jaw to pick up his car. There were a few items in the car for Anderson to dispose of.

"On the passenger side of the car, in the front seat, was a black ski jacket, or black jacket, and there was a faded pair of blue jeans there. And I left it there till I got back out to the farm, and I parked the car there and took the jacket and jeans. There was some silver, change, on the floor. There was a pair of sunglasses and there was a credit-card receipt," Anderson recalled.

Anderson also found a tuft of hair that might have come from a wig, a smear of some sort near the transmission and a pair of grey work socks. He took all of the stuff to an incinerator and destroyed it. He vacuumed his car out, and cleaned the mud off the licence plates. He and Thatcher didn't speak again for a very long time.

On January 25, JoAnn Wilson was buried. Of her three children, only Stephanie attended the funeral to say goodbye to her mother. Neither of the boys appeared.

About 400 people turned out to say goodbye to JoAnn. Among the mourners were many of the city's and the province's rich and powerful, including the attorney general, Gary Lane, and the deputy premier, Eric Berntson.

In another development that day, the city of Regina posted a $50,000 reward for information leading to the arrest and conviction of the person responsible for JoAnn's murder. Half the money was put up by the city and the other half was donated anonymously.

The day after the funeral, Thatcher received another seven roses. Later, reports would say those roses were a message from the crime underworld. They arrived at Thatcher's home in Moose Jaw accompanied by a cryptic note, which simply said, "See you around." However, the flowers were not a sign from the mob. They were traced back to a sender in Vancouver, a friend of JoAnn's, who had also been responsible for the first bouquet of red roses sent to Colin. Thatcher asked the police to lay charges, but nothing was ever done because no crime was committed.

The police investigation moved slowly but surely. On January 24, the bullet fragments were sent to the forensic science lab. On January 25, they were returned to Staff-Sergeant Somers, who started a lengthy series of tests to determine where the bullet might have come from.

Somers determined that it was probably a .38 special bullet fired from a .357 calibre handgun. He also came to the conclusion that the gun was a Ruger, which can

123

be used to fire .38 special ammunition. The bullet was very unusual in having an aluminum jacket. In the end, he decided that it was most probably a 95-grain Winchester, .38 special, plus-P, aluminum-jacketed bullet. Somers weighed the fragments, but never recorded their weight, an oversight he would later regret.

That week, the police located Jack Janzen, the owner of the J and M Shell Service Station, who had sold Colin Thatcher $29 worth of gas on January 18. Thatcher had used a government credit card, and it was an easy matter to trace the slip back. The police interviewed Janzen about half a dozen times over the next few weeks. The credit-card-slip clue was an odd fluke, because, Janzen recalls, Thatcher had started to leave without taking his copy, and Janzen had had to remind him.

On January 27, the police seized the government Oldsmobile and photographed it. They moved it to a downtown compound in Regina, where Duane Adams and Joan Hasz were asked to look at it. The car was returned to the central registry on February 11.

Meanwhile, Thatcher had decided to leave town. He flew down to Palm Springs for a short vacation. Mendell was very frightened by this point and anxious to avoid any kind of scene with Thatcher. That is why, she explains, she stayed with Thatcher for several days after the murder.

"I knew it would take several days to facilitate [moving] and get everything out, and I knew he was coming down, so I stayed while he was there and stayed while I was in the process of moving everything. I was very nervous. I wanted to be there so when he called, I would be there, and he would think everything was okay, but I wanted to get out."

Thatcher and Mendell did talk about the murder during his trip to Palm Springs, though not at once. "Even when I first met him it was apparently because

124

of the . . . supposedly because of the custody trial, and the length of time it went on, and the hassle and the press that he was convinced that his home phone in Moose Jaw had been tapped ever since then, and always, always thought it was, the whole time I knew him. And then he got into a kind of a thing where he was very paranoid about his condominium in Palm Springs being wired or bugged, and his home in Moose Jaw, even. . . . He was always telling me, you know, 'Don't say anything here.' "

They never talked about the killing inside the condominium. A few days later, however, they visited Mendell's parents. The local Palm Springs paper, *The Desert Sun*, had run an article about JoAnn's death and, as Colin and Lynne were getting into the car to go home, Lynne said, "God, you didn't, you know, you didn't tell me anything about *that*," referring to the fact that JoAnn had been viciously beaten. Thatcher replied that he didn't know why the paper had reported it, because he hadn't beaten JoAnn.

"It was a very difficult thing for me to deal with in my mind at all, totally. And I would say things like, 'I can't believe you really . . . . How did you feel?' And he said, 'Well, it's a very strange feeling to blow your wife away.' "

Lynne waited for Thatcher to leave so she could move her things out of the condominium. She feared that if she moved while he was there, he would realize how much she knew about what had gone on. She was afraid he might kill her, too.

"I don't know, there's large sliding glass doors in Palm Springs all over the condominiums and I just had a very edgy feeling at night, even sometimes during the day. I was just scared," she said.

Later that spring, Thatcher told her it had been a piece of cake, there was nothing that would let the police trace him to the murder. About five days later, when Thatcher left for Saskatchewan, Mendell went to stay with her parents.

After Thatcher left, Staff-Sergeant Beaton and a Palm Springs detective paid Lynne a surprise visit. Her father, Hank Dally, a former lawyer, had advised her to stay out of the whole mess. She realized it wasn't exactly moral advice, but that her dad was simply concerned about her well-being. So during the first interview, she didn't tell the police anything.

A few hours later, she called the station back. Officer Mike Hall informed her that they had been waiting for her call, because she was such a lousy liar. She met with the pair and told them everything she knew. Her statement was added to the lengthy file they were building on the case.

Back in Saskatchewan, the laborious process of interviewing witnesses continued. Among those interviewed was Charles Guillaume, Thatcher's former campaign manager. On March 8, the police seized the gun holster that Guillaume had found in the car Thatcher had borrowed over a year ago.

A second composite drawing of the suspect was released on February 10, using the descriptions provided by Joan Hasz and Duane Adams, in conjunction with Craig Dotson's recollection. The first wanted poster, released on January 25, had shown both a man with a moustache and a beard, and the same individual without the facial hair.

The second release, on February 10, depicted a man with much more facial hair. Everyone the police interviewed was shown the composites.

The police were under tremendous pressure. Thatcher later said that the media put so much pressure on the police to make an arrest that the police were forced to arrest him. But in reality, the police were pressuring themselves. Ed Swayze took a great deal of pride in his work. There had been only six unsolved murders in Regina in the last fifty years. He was determined to keep JoAnn Wilson's killing from becoming number seven.

Again and again, the police were drawn to Gary Anderson, particularly because one of the composite drawings resembled him. Anderson, who has had three years of post-secondary education, including a year at a Bible college, and who is not a stupid man, began to think that his 1974 Mercury was a little hot to handle. He decided to sell it.

The police also closely scrutinized Tony Wilson. Swayze interviewed Wilson at some length, simply because he had never met JoAnn and wanted to get a feel for the sort of person she was. Ed was very impressed with Tony, who, despite his attempts at a stiff upper lip, was obviously grieving deeply for his wife.

Wilson's fighting spirit was also in evidence. He continued a custody battle to keep Stephanie because he firmly believed she would have a better home with him than with her natural father. If he had won the court fight, Wilson would have done everything possible to ensure that Stephanie had a good, solid upbringing in a warm, loving home, even though he had no blood connection to the child.

Wilson actually filed an affidavit in court to prevent Colin from having any access at all to Stephanie, either before or after the custody ruling. He claims that Thatcher phoned him a week after JoAnn's murder to ask about arrangements to see Stephanie.

"I told Colin Thatcher that there was no way I was going to discuss any of these matters with the person who had arranged for the murder of my wife. Colin made no response to this assertion," Wilson recounted.

Eventually, Chief Justice Mary Batten awarded custody of Stephanie to Thatcher. Wilson was granted access to the little girl on weekends and holidays. On the advice of his lawyer, he never again publicly discussed the statements he had made in the affidavit.

Wilson wasn't the only one speaking to lawyers then. Dick Collver had once again contacted Ron Barclay to ask if he had a legal obligation to tell the police of the 1979 plot by Thatcher to hire a hit man to kill JoAnn. Once again, the advice was that he had no legal obligation to do so, and he kept silent.

In June 1983, the police investigation had a major breakthrough. Gary Anderson contacted a lawyer and said he was willing to talk about making a deal. Anderson says he spent the time from February to June doing some soul-searching. He knew that what he had done was wrong. What effect the police visits had on his conscience is not known, but presumably those visits were very persuasive.

In the months that followed, a deal was struck between the authorities and Gary Anderson. He wanted immunity from prosecution and protection if he testified. In return, he would cooperate with the police.

The deal with Gary Anderson was conditional on two things: that Anderson hadn't been physically involved in the actual killing of JoAnn Wilson; and that he tell the truth. If either of those conditions was found to have been violated, then the agreement would become void and Anderson would be open to prosecution for his involvement with the murder.

Anderson also requested that, after he completed his evidence, he would be relocated and provided with a new identity. It took from June 1983 to February 1984 to iron out the details of the agreement. Only then were the police able to get a statement from Anderson.

In the interim, however, the police located Anderson's 1974 Mercury. It had been parked behind the J and M Shell Service Station in Caron. It was seized, searched and photographed before it was returned. It's now a taxi in the city of Moose Jaw.

On March 12, 1984, Charlie Wilde found himself in

128

custody in Regina on a breach-of-probation charge. Naturally, he was questioned about his involvement with Thatcher. Wilde found himself in the holding cells with Cody Crutcher, who, like Wilde, was encouraged to tell his story.

Wilde did tell the story. As far as he was concerned, the only thing he was guilty of was fraud for misrepresenting himself to Thatcher as a gun for hire. He was in jail when JoAnn was murdered and was not implicated in her death. He, too, was promised help in changing his identity and relocating if he testified. Wilde's evidence was very damaging to Thatcher. After all, it was pointed out, if he hadn't actually met Thatcher, how else could he have known the details he did about JoAnn's family and Thatcher's yellow Corvette?

By April 1984, the Regina City Police were moving ahead with an elaborate plan. They wanted Gary to wear a body pack with a tape recorder and to meet with Colin to try to obtain a confession on tape.

To ensure that "the sting" went off without a hitch, weeks of planning went into the operation. The police carefully surveyed the abandoned farm where they believed a meeting would take place, taking both ground and aerial shots. They considered the possibility of videotaping the meeting, in case Thatcher tried to argue that the voice on the tape wasn't his. The videotape idea was dismissed as too risky, because there wasn't adequate cover in the area, and Thatcher might have noticed the camera.

By May 1, 1984, the plan was ready to take effect. The police moved a mobile trailer to Besant Regional Park, a campground a few miles from the abandoned farm. They did everything they could to ensure Gary Anderson's safety. They feared that if Thatcher smelled a set-up he might turn on Anderson and hurt their key witness.

129

Constables Ray Golemba and James McKee were part of the four-member Special Weapons and Tactics team that moved into place near the abandoned farm field at about 3:30 a.m. on the morning of May 1. They were dressed in tiger-stripe military camouflage uniforms. Their faces were smeared with two different colours of camouflage paint. That early in the year, of course, there were still few leaves on the trees, and consequently few bushes to hide behind. They used the natural protection of the tree line and some abandoned farm machinery as further camouflage.

McKee carried a .38 handgun and an M16-A1 rifle; Golemba also carried a .38 revolver, plus a .243 sniper rifle. In addition they had knives, binoculars and radio equipment. McKee had two radios — a receiver unit and a receiver-transmitter unit. Through a special earplug he was able to monitor the conversation in the yard. The men were under instructions not to give their position away unless it appeared that a threat to Anderson was imminent.

Gary Anderson arrived at the trailer park about 6 a.m. Corporal Donald Domenie of the RCMP special eye unit supervised, while a sergeant put the body pack on Anderson.

It was a tiny, sophisticated tape recorder with superior sound sensitivity. Manufactured by Nagra, a Swiss company, it was a state-of-the-art machine of a type commonly used by police forces throughout North America for this kind of operation. On this machine, there was no playback mode, which eliminated the risk of inadvertently erasing or removing a section or sections of the tape.

The machine was taped to the left side of Gary's chest, underneath a bulletproof vest. A tiny microphone — about the size of the top of a pen — was attached to the machine by a three- or four-foot cord. The microphone was placed near the hollow of Ander-

130

son's neck. On the right side of his body was taped an FM transmitter about half the size of a cigarette package. The FM transmitter, made by Bell and Howell in the States, allowed the conversation to be broadcast for backup purposes. Ed Swayze was the man listening through the headphones.

Anderson left the trailer at about 7 a.m., after being shown how to operate the machine. There was about three hours' worth of time on the tape, which was turned on just before Anderson left. He was understandably nervous, and was given instructions to keep talking to himself so that police could monitor what was happening.

Anderson left the park in his truck to look for Colin Thatcher. He found the politician fuelling up his truck and asked him if they could meet at the abandoned farm. Thatcher said, "Sure," but that he needed gas. He'd be along in a few minutes.

Thatcher looked awfully surprised to see Anderson, and for a few tense moments everyone wondered if he'd turn up.

Anderson was so nervous he was hyperventilating. For the first five or ten minutes, the tape is filled with either the sound of his breathing or his voice as he talked aloud to himself, repeating the same things over and over. He was clearly very scared as he paced back and forth waiting for Thatcher. Anderson had to be very careful with this meeting. If he pushed too hard or too far, Thatcher would simply clam up; or, worse still, he might suspect something and simply deny any knowledge of what Anderson was talking about. During Anderson's wait, the sounds of a small plane flying overhead went onto the tape. The plane contained Regina police, who were keeping an eye on the area.

Eventually, Thatcher turned up to talk to Anderson. Almost immediately, he asked if Anderson had been hassled since the murder. The pair hadn't seen each other since the afternoon Anderson turned the gun over. Thatcher noted that although the police had been trying to tie him and Anderson together, they had been unable to come up with a solid connection.

Anderson told the politician that he had disposed of the stuff he found in the Mercury, and Thatcher replied, "Good."

"You kind of give me a scare there," Anderson continued. "I found the stuff lying in there and then I wondered what the hell — I didn't know where the hell you — what the hell you'd done with the gun."

Thatcher's alarm is immediately evident in what follows: "Don't even talk like that, don't — don't even — walk out this way a little, away from the car. Now, there are no loose ends, at all, and, you know, they've gone — every which direction. Was there any way a loose end from a couple of years ago can ever resurface, from some of the guys that — discussing some business with, is there any way there's ever been a problem surface from them?" Anderson replied that he didn't think so. He knew Thatcher was referring to Wilde and Crutcher. Colin feared that if either man was picked up by the police for another crime, he might use his information on Thatcher to make a deal.

The politician asked if Anderson needed some money and the big man replied that he did, because he had had to sell his car to prevent the police from tracking it down. Thatcher agreed to leave the money in a plastic bag at the abandoned farm that Friday afternoon. He made it clear that he didn't want to meet Gary there again because he had "a great fear of those parabolic mikes".

Anderson asked Thatcher what he should do if he needed a lawyer quickly.

"Oh well, don't worry about that," Thatcher advised him. "But I mean, it ain't coming to that. It ain't

132

coming to that 'cause they have no way of — there's only two places to put the connection together, and they got zero else. They've got zero else, and I mean you know what there is to put together and it ain't possible, and it ain't coming from me. I mean, just always remember that if you were ever to say that I said this or that, it's a crock of garbage. It's just always deny, deny, deny." Thatcher went on to say that he was with four solid people the night of the killing and none of them would ever crack, including Sandra Hammond.

At that point Anderson changed the subject. "I had a hell of a time to clean the car out," he said.

"Is that right?" Thatcher replied.

"Yeah, I had a bitch of a time getting the blood and stuff off," Gary said. Thatcher then became concerned that the car might resurface, until Anderson reassured him that the car had been cleaned. Thatcher continued to stress that he didn't want to meet Anderson again unless absolutely necessary, and gave the man advice on what to say if the police did return to question him.

Anderson asked Thatcher if he still had "visions" of Ron Graham. Thatcher said he didn't, but when Anderson asked about Gerry Gerrand, JoAnn's divorce lawyer, who was intensely hated by Colin, the politician drawled out that he could "do" Gerrand. "That guy I could do," he said.

As the conversation wound down, Anderson turned one last time and said: "Yeah, I'm glad you got her."

"Okay," Thatcher replied.

While the two men were walking around the field at just after 8 a.m. that morning, they came within fifty feet of the SWAT team's position. James McKee kept his head up and observed the whole conversation. About an hour later the surveillance team came out of their hiding spots and left the field.

133

Anderson left after Thatcher, drove to the local service station and dialled Ed Swayze. He waited ten minutes, then went back to a prearranged meeting place. From that moment on, Gary was in the protective custody of the RCMP. He was moved away from his home, and his whereabouts was kept a secret. The tape was removed and three copies were made immediately and placed in different locations to protect them.

Four days later, Sergeant Jim Street went to the abandoned farm location and found a plastic bag with $550 in it, at the exact location where Thatcher had agreed to leave it.

That was also the day the abduction charges against Thatcher and Merchant were dismissed, leaving the lesser charge of mischief. Thatcher, as usual, was quite cocky about the court appearance, telling reporters outside that he didn't think he had done anything wrong.

"Any parent in Saskatchewan would have understood my actions . . . and I don't apologize for them. In the same circumstances I'd do exactly the same thing again," he said.

Regina police had a busy weekend. They were now in possession of the single most important piece of evidence they had against Thatcher — the tape of that conversation. They had to plan their next move.

On Monday, May 7, just as Thatcher reached the outskirts of Moose Jaw on the overpass, heading for the Trans-Canada Highway route to his ranch, a police car pulled up behind him and switched on its lights. Thatcher pulled over, immediately jumping from the car so that the cop wouldn't see he wasn't wearing his seatbelt. Just as the officer started to approach him, another group of policemen converged on the scene and arrested Colin for the first-degree murder of JoAnn Wilson.

Also that day, a search warrant was executed at the

Thatcher home on Redland Avenue. There the police found, in the closet in the master bedroom, a .38-calibre handgun with five rounds in it, a Sindy Shower box and a June 1982 Los Angeles newspaper. They also found two dark toques.

The Regina police had taken great care to make sure a policewoman accompanied the officers to the Redland Avenue house to tell the children of their father's arrest. The woman was there because of Stephanie. The police were surprised, even shocked, at the children's reaction. Greg immediately jumped up and ordered Regan and Stephanie not to say anything, that they didn't have to say anything without a lawyer. Stephanie stopped for a few minutes when she learned the news, but then resumed skipping around the room getting ready for school. Of necessity, it seemed, Colin Thatcher's children had become used to dealing with policemen and lawyers.

CHAPTER ELEVEN

The Trial Begins

From the second the handcuffs were snapped around Colin Thatcher's wrists that morning he ceased to be a free man. Associate Justice Minister Serge Kujawa saw to that.

Kujawa, age fifty-nine, was to prosecute the murder trial. He had stopped being a full-time Crown attorney some time before and now devoted most of his time to administration, law reform and education. He had the reputation in Saskatchewan of being his own man, of doing what he felt was right and not bending to any form of pressure.

A tall man with a figure that men several decades younger would envy, he obviously takes pains to keep himself in shape. Most of his hair has been gone for quite some time and what is left is grey. A photograph taken when he graduated from law school shows that he was thinning on top as early as age thirty-five.

His face is a little weathered, by time and living; his eyes, which are open and friendly, attract people. Kujawa's manner of speaking is simple and eloquent, and when people talk, he truly listens. It's these qualities that make him so effective with a jury.

He was three and a half when his Russian family emigrated from Poland. They settled in a small farm in the backwoods of northeast Saskatchewan. His young days in the rural school weren't easy. As a Ukrainian, he was a target for prejudice, which stayed with him until the war. After he finished his schooling, he com-

136

pleted teacher's college and taught public school for a year and a half.

In 1944, the war beckoned and he came to Regina and joined the army. He was discharged about eighteen months later and spent the next few years doing just about everything, including boxing as an amateur for a while. His next accomplishment was a law degree from the University of Saskatchewan.

A university education was then, as it is today, an expensive proposition, and he financed those years hustling pool and playing poker in the local pool hall, where a lot of small-time criminals hung out. He was thirty-five when he was admitted to the bar and spent the first eighteen months in private practice. After that he joined the attorney general's department and later became the province's first director of public prosecutions. Somehow, he found time to get married and have five daughters and a son. His daughters are his greatest cheerleaders and they attended some of Thatcher's preliminary hearing to give their dad their moral support.

In his years as a Crown attorney Kujawa prosecuted so many cases he can't keep track of them today. But it isn't the fact that he's won the majority of his cases that's remarkable. It's the man himself. If lawyers are generally thought of as long-winded and pretentious, Kujawa is certainly not typical. He's got a down-home, folksy manner about him that makes people immediately take to him and feel they can trust him.

On top of that, he's very, very bright. He and his associate, Al Johnston, worked on the case for four months before it went to trial. As the prosecutor on the abduction charges, which were dismissed, Kujawa had already been involved with the Thatcher case even before the arrest. He knows more about the Thatcher murder case than anyone in the entire world, except maybe Ed Swayze, who would give him a run for his

137

money. Kujawa's four months of preparations included coming up with every form of explanation imaginable that Thatcher might use in his own defence.

Some days, Kujawa would tell Johnston to think of possible explanations for the remarks Thatcher made on the tape. Johnston would go away, come back several hours later, start on an explanation and then realize it wouldn't work. The two men came to the conclusion as the months went by that there simply were no innocent explanations for some of the things Thatcher had said and done. Still, the Crown team had to be prepared for any eventuality. They had voice experts lined up from across the country, just in case Thatcher denied he had met Gary Anderson on May 1.

Tony Merchant represented Thatcher in his first bail application on May 8. Kujawa argued that the tape contained threats against people and that the conversation was tantamount to a murder confession. Bail was denied. When Colin's criminal lawyer, Gerry Allbright, took over the bail application an opportunity to appeal the decision was granted less than a week later but the appeal was dismissed.

Allbright, at thirty-seven, is one of the bright lights of Saskatchewan's legal community. He had got the abduction charges dismissed, and was hired immediately following the murder charges to defend Thatcher. With his neatly trimmed, reddish-brown hair, green eyes and easy smile, Allbright is the epitome of preppy good looks and exudes boyish charm.

Allbright grew up in Prince Albert, Saskatchewan, where he was strongly influenced by John Diefenbaker. "He was certainly an influence on me as a lawyer. More for what I'd call his strong courageous stand," Allbright says.

Allbright's father and grandfather were businessmen who for years operated probably the only independent grain elevator in Saskatchewan. Although

Allbright's father wasn't a lawyer, his involvement for a number of years in local politics considerably influenced Gerry's choice of career. But Gerry didn't really have any legal heroes; he feels the best thing lawyers can do is to build on their own natural style rather than try to emulate someone else's.

Allbright helped pay his way through university by joining a blues band and by playing the classical guitar. He is a keen racquetball competitor, and plays a lot at quite a high level. By 1974, just four years after he graduated from law school, Allbright was the provincial director for legal aid. He moved to defence work because he found it was more suited to his temperament.

On October 16, 1982, Allbright married Gloria Rushby, who is his secretary and receptionist. The couple celebrated their second wedding anniversary on the second day of Thatcher's murder trial. Their membership in the Pentecostal Church is a very important part of their lives.

Allbright describes the jury's role in the justice system in religious terms. He compares the jurors to the twelve disciples of Christ; in his view there is a thirteenth juror — God.

Allbright is brash and articulate; his style can sometimes seem intimidating to the person he's examining. Often he won't call a witness by name but will simply say, "Tell us what you mean, witness." Or, "Witness, can you explain yourself?" What that phraseology tends to do is depersonalize witnesses, to strip them of their identities, in a sense. It also works to remind them why they're in the courtroom in the first place.

Allbright planned another bail application for Thatcher after the preliminary hearing. That hearing started, under intense media scrutiny, on Monday, June 25, 1984, before Provincial Court Judge Marion Wedge. A ban on publication of the evidence, even of the witnesses' names, was immediately put into effect. The public turned out for the hearing in great numbers, often lining up hours before it was scheduled to start. That pattern would repeat itself at the trial later that fall.

The judge heard from twenty-five witnesses over the five-day period of the preliminary hearing. The biggest surprise — especially for Colin Thatcher — was the appearance of Lynne Mendell.

How Mendell came to appear in that Regina court-room is a story in itself. On June 5, Kujawa, Swayze and Sergeant Gene Stusek travelled to Palm Springs. They had several pieces of business to attend to on that trip. Among other things they arranged for a search warrant for Thatcher's Palm Springs condominium to see if there was any additional evidence there to link the politician to his ex-wife's murder.

The first order of business for Swayze and Kujawa was to see a judge in Palm Springs to get the search warrant for the condominium. The judge was intrigued with the information on the case. ''It sounds like the stuff movies are made of,'' he said before he granted them the warrant they needed.

Swayze and Kujawa also talked to Ron Williams, the fellow who had sold Thatcher the .357 magnum. A Canadian subpoena has no power in the United States, so if an American witness were to testify, he would have to do so voluntarily. Williams, who had been born in Canada and was a former policeman, readily agreed to appear.

Lynne Mendell was something different. She had much more to lose than Ron Williams. She had married the summer before and wanted to put Colin Thatcher out of her life forever. To come back to testify against him could put her in danger and open up her life to public scrutiny, to say nothing of reviving unpleasant memories.

Mendell met with Swayze and Kujawa privately first. She left them saying she wanted to talk to her husband, Bill Mendell, an ABC-TV executive in Palm Springs. The couple returned to the hotel the next day at 4 p.m.

Kujawa and Swayze were nervously awaiting the Mendells' arrival. They weren't relying on Mendell's evidence to make the case, but she would be helpful in putting a few more nails into Thatcher's coffin. Although they didn't know what the outcome of the meeting would be, oddly enough both men had a feeling that Mendell would agree to testify. They had no recourse if she refused — there was no way they could force her to appear.

Just after 4 p.m., the Mendells sat down and listened seriously to what Kujawa and Swayze had to say. Bill Mendell turned to his wife and told her it was her own decision, and that whatever she chose to do, he would stand by her.

Lynne walked to the window and stared outside for a few minutes. The men waited anxiously for her decision. When she turned and quietly said she would testify, her husband stood up to embrace her. After a tender moment with his wife, Mendell turned to Kujawa and Swayze and made an impassioned speech, which Kujawa says he will never forget.

Mendell spoke simply about the moral obligation his wife had to protect our way of life, to protect society against people like Colin Thatcher and to do her bit to keep society civilized.

When he was finished, Kujawa said he felt like saluting Mendell and standing to attention to sing ''God Bless America''. Later, when they were discussing security for Lynne, they had to tell her that there was nothing they could do to protect her in Palm Springs, although they would do everything they could to ensure her safety while she was in Canada.

Lynne became a little frightened at that point, but her husband reminded her: "Yes, but we're talking about murder here, Lynne."

Kujawa has a great deal of respect for Lynne Mendell. "She's a very courageous woman," he says. He knows she could very easily have refused to become involved and saved herself a lot of the personal grief attached to having the most intimate moments of her life dredged up in court. She had nothing to gain; she had started a new life with a new man, and she could have opted to keep her life simple.

Lynne's explanation of why she agreed to testify is straightforward. For starters, she claims she never would have gone if Bill had not been so supportive. But also, she did feel she had a moral obligation to testify. "It's the fine line that makes us civilized," she says simply. "I had to do it."

When Swayze and Kujawa left Palm Springs, they asked Lynne if she had any conditions for her security or appearance as a witness. She jokingly told them she had to be picked up at the airport in a Mercedes driven by a handsome young man. The two men exchanged looks and smiled. What Mendell didn't know is that Swayze, who was going to escort her from the airport, drives a silver Mercedes.

Mendell slipped into Regina under tight security for the preliminary hearing, which was held to determine whether there was enough evidence to send Thatcher to trial. Her presence was a complete surprise to Allbright and Thatcher. It had never occurred to Colin that Mendell would turn against him. Whenever he had seen her in Palm Springs, she had seemed friendly, and when she had met his new girlfriend, Diane Stoner, a Regina nurse, she had told Thatcher to hang onto her because she seemed very nice. In actual fact, Mendell was afraid of Colin and was trying to stay on his good side.

142

The following months weren't easy for Lynne. "I'd wake up in the middle of the night and look at my husband and start crying because I was scared," she said.

Her fears were fuelled by two anonymous phone calls. The first was in August 1984. A male voice told her that this time it was a friendly call, but that "we're going to get both you and your husband. Remember, we're never very far away. You're playing in the big leagues now." Lynne phoned Bill right away. Bill called Ed Swayze, Swayze called Lynne back and calmed her down.

The second call came about ten days before the trial. The man's voice was different, but the message was the same. "If you go north we'll take both you and your husband out," the voice warned.

"I knew they didn't mean for dinner," Mendell recalls. Again a call was placed to Swayze to say that she had great fears about testifying. Swayze, who had now been promoted to deputy-chief of the Regina police force, phoned Lynne every day after that to talk to her.

In retrospect, it's a good thing there were only two phone calls. If she had received daily calls, Mendell claims today, she would not have testified. Lynne Mendell was one of twenty-five witnesses at the five-day preliminary hearing.

Judge Marion Wedge wasted no time at the end of the evidence. She declined to give the reasons for her decision, saying that that was the first bit of advice she'd ever received as a judge. "Having carefully considered the evidence as I went along, I'm not going to adjourn to review what I have decided is proper for me to do in this case.

"If you'll stand up, Mr. Thatcher, I find that there is sufficient evidence to commit you for trial. You are therefore committed for trial, at a judge and jury sitting, of course, of the Queen's Bench Court in Regina," she said.

Thatcher took the decision very calmly and was whisked away by waiting officers. He didn't stop to speak to one of his sons, who had rushed to the front of the court to have a few words with his dad.

The next order of business for Gerry Allbright was to make a bail application on Colin's behalf again. That application was turned down on July 18. Once again, the judge placed a ban on the reasons for denying bail.

Allbright won a battle in August. He applied to have the location of the trial changed because of extensive publicity. Although a publication ban had been placed on all the evidence from the preliminary hearing, a number of Regina residents had ordered copies of the transcript, at $153 a copy, photocopied them and started passing them around. This gave Allbright a good argument for having the trial moved to a city where less was known about the events. Conveniently for Allbright, the city selected was Saskatoon, where his office and home are.

On September 9, bail was denied Thatcher for the fourth time. It was becoming plain that he would be in custody until after the trial, which was scheduled to begin on October 15. On that same day, Thatcher was rushed to the hospital in an ambulance, suffering from chest pains. He had been having problems with his heart and was taking medication. He was held overnight for tests while Regina Correctional Centre guards kept him under a watchful eye. He returned to the jail on September 11.

The weekend before the trial, journalists from all across the country began to arrive in Saskatoon. Arrangements had been made for members of the press to apply for seats in the courtroom, which could accommodate only 112 people. Initially, twenty-eight seats were set aside for the media, but that number was bumped to thirty on the Friday before the trial and later to thirty-five, after Chief Justice Mary Batten discovered that journalists who hadn't been able to get seats were buying them from the public.

The press occupied the first two rows of seats in the courtroom and part of the fourth row. It stuck in Thatcher's craw that the press had the best seats while his family had to share the third row with the bar association and the law students. Through Greg, at nineteen now the head of the Thatcher household, Colin fought determinedly to have his supporters moved to the front row. (Greg had been supervising the ranch and farming operations since his father's arrest, while Sandra Silversides, Thatcher's constituency secretary, was doing what she could to serve the constituents of Thunder Creek riding, for which Thatcher was technically still the sitting PC member.)

Thatcher's family arrived in Saskatoon just before the trial began, checking into the Ramada Renaissance, just across from the back alley of the courthouse. With the Crown, the police, the witnesses, the justice officials, many of the press and the Thatchers all staying at the hotel, the next three weeks promised some interesting encounters in the hotel elevators, lobby and swimming pool.

Thatcher's mother, Peggy, was in court every day to support her son. Thatcher's oldest son, Greg, and Diane, Thatcher's girlfriend, were regulars, too. Colin's other children, Regan and Stephanie, were to join the family members after the initial evidence was put in.

Stephanie's appearance at the trial angered and offended many people. The little girl is a beautiful child with a halo of golden curls and big hazel eyes. Although she wasn't there to hear the pathological evidence of how her mother met her death, she was in court the day Thatcher admitted to adultery — among other unsavoury facts of the unhappy marriage.

Stephanie was so small she had to borrow the bulky coat of an RCMP officer to sit on so that she could see the proceedings. On days when it was particularly crowded, she sat on Greg's lap and watched. For much of the time she was absorbed in Nancy Drew mystery books, and seemed oblivious to what was being said.

The person probably most bothered by Stephanie's presence was Serge Kujawa. With six children of his own, he had definite opinions about what was appropriate for a child, and a little girl's attendance at her father's murder trial didn't fit into the "appropriate" category.

Although he didn't change his strategy on her account, Stephanie's presence did make both Kujawa and his co-counsel, Al Johnston, also father of small children, uneasy. Deputy-Chief Swayze pointed out that it was illegal to have a child that age out of school. He, too, was bothered by her presence.

Stephanie made friends among the people around her. It was impossible not to like her. One afternoon she asked one of the media courtroom artists if she could look at his work. She explained that she was taking art courses and was interested. He quickly ripped off the top sheet and gave her a clean piece of paper and a marker. She sat down and drew an excellent sketch of a unicorn, signed the sketch and dated it, while her grandmother looked on proudly. Stephanie's artistic streak was probably inherited from her mother, from whom she'd also obviously inherited her looks. All of the Thatcher children are bright and attractive.

The trial ran over Hallowe'en night. Duane Smith, the security guard at the back door of the courthouse, wanted to help Stephanie celebrate Hallowe'en in a normal fashion, despite the sobering reality of her fam-

146

ily situation. He arranged for Stephanie to go trick-or-treating with his eight-year-old daughter. The two little girls immediately got into a somewhat heated discussion over the rival merits of a teddy-bear costume as opposed to a Cabbage Patch Doll costume. For a few hours, anyway, Stephanie was able to enjoy an ordinary good time, away from the curious eye of the cameras.

Stephanie is a very bright little girl, too, who probably understood too much of the tragic drama for her own good. One day during a break, while Allbright was talking to the family, Stephanie looked up and asked: ''Are we going to win this one?'' Allbright just smiled at her and continued talking to the older family members.

Many people believe Thatcher was simply using the child to gain sympathy with the jury. However, it may have been right for her to be with her family at such a difficult time. Being left behind in Moose Jaw while the rest of the family attended the trial might have been hard on her. Wherever she was, it would have been next to impossible to shield her from news reports or the comments of the other children at school. At least, this way, she heard the evidence first-hand while her grandmother or someone else who loved her was there to explain it in terms she could understand.

JoAnn's parents, Harlan and Betty Geiger, didn't come to the trial, although they had considered doing so. They had lost their daughter many years before, when she married Colin. The trial would have been too painful.

The Thatcher murder trial was billed as the biggest in the west since Louis Riel. The public had a tremendous interest in it and lined up every morning and every afternoon for the roughly sixty-five available seats. At the height of it all, while Thatcher was on the

147

witness stand, the line-up started at 2 a.m. when the temperature was $-26°C$. And the Saskatoon City Police had to be called in one lunch hour to control the crowd, after two women had a loud argument.

Everyone was searched with a metal detector before being allowed to enter the courtroom. For his protection, Thatcher was to sit in a prisoner's box—brought in specially for him—at the side of the court, instead of in the regular one, which is placed so that the accused faces the judge, with his back to the crowd. For almost all of the trial, however, Thatcher shared the counsel table with Gerry Allbright.

Mr. Justice J. H. Maher was the judge assigned to the case. He's one of the most popular judges in Saskatchewan's legal community and one of the most experienced. He had a sense of humour, and a light touch with the jury. He provided the leadership they looked for when they started their difficult task.

What makes a trial like this so fascinating? Kujawa said later he thinks it's because there is nothing more compelling than the spectacle of interesting people in trouble. Many people believed Thatcher would never be convicted because of who he was; still more people believed he'd never get a fair trial because of the extensive publicity. Here was a chance to put the jury system to work and see if it was fair.

The day the trial started was so bright and warm that the lawyers walked to the court without overcoats, carrying their gowns in plastic bags. The good weather lasted exactly one day. Overnight, Saskatoon was hit with one of the worst snowstorms ever, with temperatures colder for the time of year than they'd been since almost the beginning of the century. It was as though something evil had blown into town and the wind was the Devil's own breath. It stayed that way until the trial was over.

Colin Thatcher is led by the RCMP to the jury selection in Saskatoon on October 15.

Judge J.H. Maher of the Saskatchewan Court of Queen's Bench leaving court.

Ed Swayze, the chief police investigator.

Crown prosecutor Serge Kujawa arriving at the court for the second day of witness testimony.

Defence lawyer Gerry Allbright arriving with Greg Thatcher *(centre)*.

People lined up in freezing weather to get one of the 70 seats available to the general public.

Lynne Mendell is escorted under high security to testify in the Thatcher trial.

Sandra Silversides, Thatcher's housekeeper who testified he was at home the night of the murder.

Crown witness Tony Wilson, husband of JoAnn, after his testimony.

Former Conservative leader Dick Collver was a surprise Crown witness.

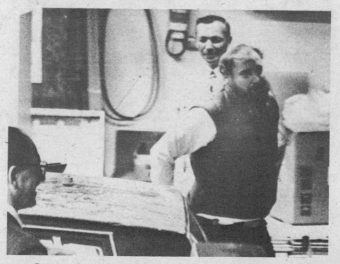

Gary Anderson, a key Crown witness, avoided the media throughout his testimony.

October 23 was the first time the immediate Thatcher family
appeared at the trial. From left to right, Greg, Stephanie, mother
Peggy and Regan.

CHAPTER TWELVE

The Prosecution

To everyone's surprise the trial got off to a quick start. By the end of the first day the jury had been selected, Kujawa had completed his opening address and the jury had heard from four witnesses.

The jury selection took less than forty minutes. Fifty-seven people were called, but the seven-man, five-woman jury was made up after only thirty-six candidates had been seen. Before each person was even considered, Mr. Justice Maher asked whether he or she had read the transcript of the preliminary hearing, was a relative of Thatcher or his family, or was related to any of the possible witnesses. None of them was. All fifty-seven candidates were present when the formal indictment was read to Thatcher and he pleaded "not guilty" to the charge. Of the thirty-six potential jurors called, Allbright challenged or vetoed sixteen of them, among them twelve women. Kujawa asked eight others, four of them women, to stand aside.

Mr. Justice Maher ruled that the jury wouldn't be sequestered for the trial, but ordered them not to talk to anyone about the evidence and advised them not to read the newspapers or follow the radio and television reports of the trial.

Allbright asked that the jurors' identities and occupations be placed under a publication ban. They were warned to be wary of anyone who tried to approach them about the trial process, and the judge asked them to report anything untoward to the court immediately.

The trial was ready to begin.

Kujawa took his place at the podium in front of the jury to start his opening address. The Crown's case, he said, could be divided into four different parts, each on its own enough to justify laying the charge against Colin Thatcher.

Part one, the physical side of the case, would include evidence relating to: the suspicious car that neighbours saw outside Wilson's house the week of the murder; the gun holster discovered inside a car that Thatcher had signed out some time before the murder; and the unusual bullet that was used to kill JoAnn.

Part two of the evidence would be direct testimony by a former girlfriend of Thatcher's who had given information about the killing.

Part three would be the evidence of Gary Anderson, who would tell the jury how he had refused to kill Wilson but had agreed to provide Thatcher with a car, ammunition and leads to people who might be willing to do the job for him.

Part four would be the tape of the conversation between Anderson and Thatcher. Kujawa told the jury he planned to call a total of twenty-eight witnesses to testify against the politician.

Then they moved directly into the evidence. The first witness was Constable Walter Brian Fryklund, whose photographs of the Wilson house and JoAnn's body were entered as exhibits. He stated that he had tested the credit-card receipt for fingerprints but had found only those of two policemen.

Craig Dotson testified next. He told the jury about the wild, shrill screams he had heard after passing the Wilson house that night. Dotson described seeing a man leave the garage. But he said he saw him only for an instant in darkness at a distance and had no interest in him at the time. Under cross-examination by

Allbright, Dotson admitted that he had seen the killer for only "one second, two seconds, maybe three seconds". He also admitted that the man he had described to the police that night didn't look like Colin Thatcher but added that he was not satisfied with the description he gave at that time or now.

Corporals Edward Pearson and Donald Bird took the witness stand that afternoon and described the items they had found in Thatcher's house during the search on May 7, 1984. The Sindy Shower box and the June 1982 *Los Angeles Times* were both entered as exhibits that day. The explanation of their significance was to follow, as Kujawa carefully unveiled his case over the next week and a half.

Court finished that day on an optimistic note. A great deal of ground had been covered very quickly. Perhaps the trial would not last the estimated three weeks, after all.

At the Ramada Renaissance, an elaborate system of security had been set up for the protection of the Crown witnesses. The Regina police had booked the entire nineteenth floor of the hotel — the top floor, for security reasons. The corner unit, which overlooked the courthouse, was occupied by policemen who watched the comings and goings down the back alley of the building. Kujawa had the presidential suite, which included a bar, living area, dining area and sunken bathtub. Swayze had similar digs down the hall. The security system included mirrors placed at the turnings of the corridors so that police could monitor anyone coming or going anywhere in the hallways.

The security system had been set up chiefly to protect key witnesses like Mendell, Wilde and Anderson. Reporters who ventured onto the floor in search of juicy tidbits were quickly escorted to the elevator. The cops stayed in touch with one another by means of a two-way radio system. A portion of the bottom floor of the hotel garage was also blocked off, to enable witnesses to be moved in and out in vans. And the vans had dark-tinted windows to prevent photographers from getting clear pictures. The elevators were equipped with a key that could be turned to prevent them from stopping anywhere except the nineteenth floor.

Overnight the snowstorm hit. Saskatoon was virtually paralysed. All incoming and outgoing flights had to stop for the next day and a half, and the city spent half its snow-removal budget for the year in that one week. Because one of the jurors lived outside of Saskatoon, Mr. Justice Maher adjourned court early that day.

The next morning, Constable Joe Fraser described for the jury the scene that had greeted him that night in January 1983. He testified that he was first on the scene and that he then stood watch outside the Wilson garage until JoAnn's body was removed to the morgue for the autopsy.

Constable Thomas Schuck then described finding the credit-card slip lying in the snow. On cross-examination, Allbright queried him closely. "If somebody had wanted you and your colleagues to find it, they couldn't have left it in a better place," the lawyer suggested. When Schuck agreed, Allbright went a step further. "Do you get the feeling someone almost left a calling card?" he asked. This time Schuck replied no.

Sergeant Bob Murton, the investigating officer on the scene that night, told the jury that the signature on the credit-card slip looked like "Thatch", and verified that he had turned it over to Fryklund of the identification bureau for fingerprint testing. He also reported having received a length of pipe from Gary Anderson many months after the murder. This piece of evidence would be explained later.

A trial is much like a jigsaw puzzle with the pieces carefully placed face down. The jurors never get a total picture until all the evidence has been presented. In order to keep continuity of exhibits, too, occasionally the evidence is called out of sequence. But Kujawa maintained a brisk pace and the jurors were never left in the dark for too long.

Jack Janzen, the owner of the J and M Shell station, was called to give evidence next. He was able to tell the jury that Thatcher was a regular customer and that he purchased gas on January 18, as the receipt indicated. The receipt had Colin's name on it with his vehicle licence number. Janzen also testified that the signature resembled Thatcher's. Under cross-examination, he admitted to Allbright that Thatcher might simply have thrown the receipt into his truck and left it lying there.

Allbright, too, was laying the groundwork for his defence. Although explanatory evidence for the proximity of the credit-card receipt was never really offered, it was the position of the defence that Thatcher wouldn't have been stupid enough to leave the receipt, like a calling card, at a murder scene for the police to find. Thatcher testified later that since he often left his truck open, it would have been easy for someone to steal the credit-card slip. The defence would allege later that the receipt could have been planted on the snowbank by the true killer, in an attempt to frame Thatcher.

The next three witnesses to testify were the three neighbours who had observed the blue Oldsmobile outside the Wilson home the week of the murder.

Joan Hasz described how the car had bothered her that week and how she had driven home repeating the numbers "292" over and over. When her family had asked her what was wrong, she had told them: "If anything goes wrong, remember those numbers."

Margaret Johannsson didn't have as much information to offer as Hasz or Duane Adams. Johannsson confirmed that the blue car she had seen did look like the one in the police photographs, but she hadn't actually been able to observe the driver as closely as Hasz and Adams had done.

Both Hasz and Adams described the driver of the suspicious car as a man with a dark, well-trimmed beard, wearing tight surgical-type gloves. Both estimated the man's age at about thirty. (Thatcher was forty-four at the time of the killing.)

Under cross-examination, Adams testified that the driver did not look like the accused.

Hasz and Adams had been able to pick the car out of the parking compound when they were taken there separately by Regina police. Hasz remembered a black-and-yellow sticker on the bumper.

One witness couldn't give her evidence that day because of the bad weather. Allbright and Kujawa agreed that Linda McKay's affidavit as given at the preliminary hearing could be entered in lieu of her giving evidence in person.

An employee of the Central Vehicle Agency of the Saskatchewan government, McKay had testified at the preliminary hearing that Thatcher had signed out a blue 1980 four-door Oldsmobile on January 10, 1983. That car, too, had had a black-and-yellow government sticker on it.

By three o'clock, when court adjourned for the day, the jury had heard from eleven witnesses in person and one through an admission, in two days of court hearings.

Thatcher had appeared very relaxed during those two days. He winked confidently at Greg when he walked into the courtroom on his first day, a practice he was to repeat over the next few weeks.

The third day of evidence opened with Charles Guillaume describing the holster he had found in the government car and Thatcher's reaction to its appearance. Under cross-examination, Guillaume admitted that Thacher hadn't appeared the least bit concerned when shown the holster.

Sergeant Gene Leonard Stusek testified next, and through him Kujawa admitted the photographs of the blue Oldsmobile that had been taken outside Thatcher's Moose Jaw home two days after the shooting. Stusek also described the search of the Palm Springs condominium. They had been looking for guns, ammunition or a running shoe with a print similar to the one found in the snow outside the Wilson garage. Nothing had been found at the condominium, Stusek said.

The next witness was a major one. Lynne Mendell, wearing grey suede boots, a grey skirt, a brown turtleneck sweater and a grey tweed jacket, stepped into the witness box and took her oath to tell the truth.

Her most jarring evidence concerned the statement she said Thatcher had made to her that, "I have to admit it's a strange feeling blowing your wife away." That line made headlines all across the country.

Mendell was calm and self-assured as she testified in her soft, breathy voice. She told the jury that Thatcher had frequently talked about killing JoAnn as a way out of his problems, and described his intense hatred of his former wife and his evident bitterness over the divorce settlement. She discussed the first shooting of JoAnn and Thatcher's report that he had staked out an area from which he could fire the rifle into the kitchen and strike her. The jury was riveted during her evidence and paid close attention to every word. Mendell wanted to give evidence about the incident at the Savoy in London during her trip to Europe with Thatcher, but the opportunity didn't come during examination-in-chief and Allbright steered away from the topic in his cross-examination.

Gerry Allbright can be unrelenting in cross-examination and he was waiting to get at Mendell. Destroying Mendell's credibility was the only way of discrediting her direct evidence of Thatcher's involvement in the crime.

Allbright suggested that Mendell was putting on a fine act for the jury and that she was actually enjoying the notoriety the trial was bringing her.

"The life of my husband and myself has been threatened twice by telephone," she snapped back. "Do you think I enjoy it?"

He pressed her again and again about why she had never notified the police before the murder occurred. "You had the chance to prevent the taking of a human life and you passed it up with a snap of the fingers, isn't that it?" Allbright asked.

"If that's the way you want to put it. I don't put it that way," she replied. "Perhaps it was a mistake," she said later.

Allbright wheeled and asked her at one point why she continued to see Thatcher after the murder. "Witness, what kind of a woman sleeps with a man she is not married to when she knows in her mind that man has just committed murder?" he demanded.

"Someone who is afraid if she didn't . . . she would get smacked around again," Mendell replied. Earlier the jury had heard her tell how she had packed her bags and left Thatcher several times during their stormy, two-year relationship.

Allbright was pacing the courtroom, sometimes completely turning his back to Mendell and staring out over the heads of the spectators. He tended to do this when he was trying to decide where to go next with a witness. Sometimes the expression on a spectator's face would give him a feeling for the mood in the courtroom.

Allbright turned and asked Mendell if she thought she was an emotionally stable person and she answered, "Yes".

Raising his voice almost to a shout, Allbright demanded: "Do emotionally stable people attempt to commit suicide?"

Mendell explained again that she had taken the

292s after arguing with Thatcher over his repeatedly broken promise to marry her.

Allbright then accused Mendell of resenting JoAnn and hating her. "You resented that lady being Mrs. Thatcher because she prevented *you* from being Mrs. Thatcher, with the first-class trips and the lands," Allbright said.

Mendell denied it, but said that marriage certainly was an issue between her and Colin, both because he had promised it and because it was not unusual for marriage to be discussed between a man and a woman.

Allbright finally accused her of fabricating her testimony to get back at Thatcher for not marrying her.

Mendell's response was that if she had been only fabricating the story, the calls threatening her life and her husband's life would have been enough to prevent her from testifying. "It would have been the easiest option to stay in Palm Springs and not attend this trial," she said.

The defence tried to make out that Mendell was not a reliable witness because she bore Thatcher rancour for not marrying her. Thatcher was later to tell the jury that Mendell was a typical child of the sixties, who'd "had some interesting experiences with soft drugs."

Despite the fact that Mendell was under heavy security and the judge had forbidden anyone to talk to the witnesses during the trial, the press was clamouring for a photograph of Lynne.

Consequently, she agreed to a short photo-session outside the back of the courtroom. It was one way of ensuring that she wouldn't be hounded for the rest of her stay in Saskatoon. Thatcher had watched her testimony with interest, dividing his attention between Mendell and the jury to see what effect her evidence was having on them. Thatcher's mother, Peggy, sat motionless while Lynne divulged some of the more intimate details of the affair.

Mendell was whisked back to the hotel that night,

again under heavy guard, before her return to Palm Springs. Her husband had wanted to be by her side during the trial, but work obligations had prevented it. When she got back to Palm Springs he told her he admired her courage and said he didn't think he'd have had the guts to do what she'd done.

Mendell was to stay in touch with Swayze and Kujawa for the next couple of weeks to keep abreast of the progress of the trial. Of all the witnesses, she had the largest stake in the outcome, since she had reason to fear what might happen to her if Thatcher became a free man.

The next morning, Dr. John Vetters took the witness stand. His evidence was horrifying. For the first time, the terror of JoAnn Wilson's last five minutes of life was made public. It focused attention, soberingly, on the very real human tragedy of JoAnn Wilson, at least temporarily diverting people's minds from the issue of who and what Colin Thatcher is.

Vetters explained the injuries in a clinical fashion, describing how many wounds there were, their length and what, in his opinion, had caused them.

He told the shocked courtroom that he couldn't tell if the twenty-seven wounds, or groups of wounds, would alone have been sufficient to kill JoAnn. The bullet to the head was the official cause of death. That bullet had also caused a skull fracture, which ran from the entry point of the bullet to the base of the brain. It was impossible to tell what damage the beating did to her brain, because the bullet had exploded into at least fourteen fragments inside her head. In addition, the pathologist said, there were cuts on her face so severe that they would have required sutures. Those cuts probably occurred when her face struck the floor after she was shot.

Staff-Sergeant Arnold Somers of the RCMP forensic science unit testified next. Somers told the jury he believed the bullet that killed JoAnn to have been a .38-special (which is the same size as a .357) bullet, weighing 95 grains, with an unusual aluminum jacket, a hollow point and a silver tip. Somers said he believed the bullet was made exclusively by Winchester, a U.S. company. He also thought the bullet was "plus-P" — that is, reserved for police use. "It would not be available on the retail market in Canada for just anyone to buy over the counter," he said.

Allbright was ready for Somers on the cross-examination. He asked him specifically how many grains the bullet fragments taken from JoAnn's body had weighed. Somers replied that he had weighed them during the tests but hadn't recorded the actual weight. Without the weight, Allbright argued, the calibre of the bullet could not be accurately determined. The bullet could easily have come from a variety of guns of a lower calibre. (Calibre refers to the gun barrel's diameter. The smaller the calibre, the smaller the bullet, and the less it weighs.)

On re-examination, a scale was brought into the courtroom and the fragments were weighed. They weighed 83.6 grains (7,000 grains equals one pound). Somers testified that he believed the fragments he'd been unable to remove from the heavy bone behind JoAnn's eye, when added to the 83.6 grains, would have made a 95-grain bullet.

Allbright wasn't finished with Somers. He took issue with Somers's claim that that type of bullet was not available for retail purchase in Canada. Allbright brought out three boxes of ammunition, purchased at a Drinkwater, Saskatchewan, gun shop, that were very similar, if not identical, to the type of ammunition Somers had said could not be legally purchased in Canada.

The RCMP officer said that he had based his statement on information from officials at the ammunition

169

manufacturing plant in the United States and RCMP laboratories in Vancouver and Winnipeg.

Next, Ron Williams, the gun salesman from Palm Springs, took the stand. He was a straightforward witness who produced documents to show that Thatcher had bought his .357 Ruger revolver on January 29, 1982 and picked it up around February 20, along with two boxes of ammunition.

Williams testified that he had sold Thatcher Winchester Western, .38-special, plus-P, silver-tipped, aluminum-jacketed bullets. His evidence was not challenged, and the next witness was Tony Wilson, the dead woman's husband.

Wilson, too, was straightforward in his story. He detailed some of the problems JoAnn had had with Thatcher during the time they were married. "They were ongoing; they were on all the time. She was in court all the time," Wilson told the jury.

The court heard how Thatcher was supposed to pay $87,500 in February 1983, only weeks after JoAnn was killed. Wilson also mentioned the clause in the contract providing that if she died Thatcher didn't have to make a payment for another year. Wilson said that he hadn't received any money from Thatcher, although as executor of JoAnn's estate he would be going after the money. At the time of JoAnn's death, Thatcher had owed $350,000. JoAnn's will stipulated that Stephanie was to get $250,000, Tony $70,000 and JoAnn's parents $30,000.

The steel-company executive described both the shooting and the murder of his wife in calm, subdued terms.

Allbright's cross-examination was aggressive. He even went so far as to ask Tony if he had killed JoAnn himself for the $70,000. That suggestion was a little odd, considering that Wilson's annual salary from IPSCO is more than that, and that his wife, had she lived, had

170

another $350,000 coming to her. At any rate, Wilson very calmly replied, "Of course not," to Allbright's question.

Allbright threw a little bit of mud Wilson's way. He wanted to know why the housekeeper, Maria Lahtinen, was still living in the Wilson house, although Stephanie had returned to her natural father. Wilson had the house up for sale, but he, his son and Lahtinen were still in residence. The woman was obviously no longer needed as Stephanie's baby-sitter, but was a university student and Wilson had allowed her to continue living in the house.

Allbright wanted to know if the young housekeeper had been causing marital difficulties between JoAnn and Tony.

"I would say it was all nonsense," Wilson said, appearing insulted. "She's a student. We have a large house and there's no reason to throw her out."

Allbright accused Wilson of continuing to go after the property settlement out of "spite".

"I'm following her instructions," Wilson replied. As JoAnn's executor, he knows how his wife wanted the settlement divided.

Allbright finished his cross-examination by saying to Wilson: "You wouldn't mind seeing Colin Thatcher convicted, would you?"

"No, I would not mind," came the simple reply.

Day five of the trial opened with an admission by Allbright. It was from the owner of the gun shop where Allbright had purchased the ammunition. In a statement read out in court, owner Clint Sandborn admitted that he had gone to the Red Rock Sporting Goods Store in Miles, Montana, to buy the ammunition that Allbright had ordered on October 10, five days before the trial started. The ammunition had had to be cleared at Canadian customs and was subsequently sold to Gerry.

To further drive the point home, Kujawa called customs officer Larry Piller to the stand.

Piller remembered Sandborn and two other men crossing through his station with $383.17 worth of ammunition that day. The ammunition, when checked with the broker's itemized list, matched the record of ammunition that had been imported.

Piller told the jury that most hollow-point ammunition cannot be imported into Canada unless it is used for a .22-calibre rifle, or is to be sold to police forces by licensed gun dealers.

On cross-examination, Allbright slapped down another box of ammunition. The box had fifty shells of Winchester .357, 145-grain, silver-tipped, hollow-point bullets. He had a receipt from the Saskatoon Gun Works. As an aside to the jury, Allbright added: "I'm going broke buying this stuff."

Allbright then asked Piller if he could be wrong about what kind of ammunition was allowed into Canada to be sold. Piller replied he'd gotten his information from a memo at the customs office dealing with hollow-point bullets.

"I'm as certain as I can be," he told the defence lawyer.

The two debated for a few minutes about whether the ammunition had been properly or improperly sold, until Justice Maher intervened to say that the customs officer shouldn't have to worry about whether the dealers were breaking the law by selling the ammunition.

"His [Piller's] knowledge ends at the border," the judge said.

Piller's examination ended at about 11:30 a.m. Kujawa then rose to his feet to apologize, saying that the next witness was unavailable to testify. He asked if they could break for the weekend.

Gerry Allbright reacted quickly. He jumped to his feet and addressed the judge. "Colin Thatcher's been in custody for six months," he objected. "The jury's here, we're here. . . . I'd like this case to come to a conclusion."

Kujawa apologized again, and offered to call evidence to explain why the witness was mysteriously unavailable. "I don't mind being part of a new low," he retorted.

Outside the courtroom, he apologized to the reporters clamouring to know the details of Gary Anderson's disappearance. "I expect him to be in court at 10 a.m. on Monday," Kujawa simply said.

The failure of Gary Anderson to appear sparked rumours that persisted and grew all through the weekend. He'd been killed; he'd committed suicide; his body had been found floating in the South Saskatchewan River, the rumours went. The rumour that came closest to the truth was that he was in police custody after threatening someone with a gun.

The burly key witness had been in partial protective custody since the day of the taped conversation. The RCMP had relocated him and kept his whereabouts a secret. But in the months before his appearance in court, Anderson decided he didn't like the way he'd been treated. He said he'd been constantly harassed and bothered during the procedures for getting him things like a driver's licence, a new social insurance number and new medical documents.

"It's my opinion that the RCMP in Regina just didn't give a shit about it," he said later.

At the beginning of September, Anderson had left the place where he was staying and gone to his mother's farm in Caron.

He had become depressed and lonely in his new location and had just wanted to return to his home turf.

Anderson had driven himself to Saskatoon on the Monday the trial started, but became angry and upset with the police. He returned to Caron and phoned Ed Swayze, telling him that, "If he wanted me, he could darn well come down and get me."

The police did go down to the farm. (Kujawa had been there to see Anderson on another occasion, and described the yard as a desolate and lonely place, like something out of a Thomas Hardy novel. On that occasion, Anderson, who was slightly paranoid about his role in the trial, had come running down from the house to see what Kujawa wanted. The two men had stood nose to nose for a second and then Anderson, who weighs about 230 pounds, said to Kujawa: "What are you smirking about?"

"I was just thinking to myself," Kujawa had said calmly, "that I wish you were about one hundred pounds lighter."

Anderson had stared at Kujawa for a second, then burst into a belly laugh.)

Unfortunately, the situation faced by the Regina police was not so easily defused. After the phone call to Swayze, Anderson had holed himself up in the house with his girlfriend and his shotgun. He had already pulled the gun out about a month before when he discovered a conservation officer from Moose Jaw on his land. On the Thursday, he started taking Tylenol pills for the severe headaches he was getting. He took about twelve during the day, and swallowed another twenty-four after dinner. Among the policemen who helped surround the farmhouse to try to talk Gary Anderson out was Sergeant Jim Street. As Street had left the hotel in Saskatoon he'd said to Kujawa: "I don't think he'll shoot me, Serge." Showing considerable courage, Street walked up to the door of Anderson's farmhouse and persuaded Anderson to let him in. The reluctant witness, who was sitting at the table, wouldn't allow Street to come much past the threshold. They talked for a while; then Anderson told Street to leave the house.

Later that night, the police phoned Anderson's girlfriend and told her the house was surrounded. When he eventually came out and surrendered, Anderson spent some time in the hospital and the rest of it in a police barracks until it was time for him to testify.

On Monday morning, October 22, Anderson stepped into the witness box to tell the jury of his long involvement with Colin Thatcher before the murder of JoAnn.

He detailed the early meetings — Thatcher's offer of $50,000 if Anderson would kill JoAnn, Anderson's refusal and his counter-offer to put Thatcher in touch with someone who would. Anderson described the meetings with Charlie Wilde and Cody Crutcher and gave details of the money he had received from Thatcher to pay them. The jury heard about the first shooting attempt. Anderson recalled asking Thatcher how he could have missed Wilson at that range. Anderson described how he and Dan Doyle had made the silencers for the gun; then he identified the piece of pipe submitted as an exhibit after Sergeant Murton's testimony as one of the silencers that he had retrieved from a field and given to Murton.

Finally, Anderson described the efforts he had made to clean the car out, removing the clothing Thatcher had left and any other evidence that might link the former cabinet minister to the murder of his wife.

After lunch, Kujawa asked for a break in Anderson's testimony to introduce Corporal Donald Domenie. Domenie described how he had wired Gary Anderson for sound before the conversation with Thatcher on the morning of May 1.

There was some discussion about whether Anderson had freely consented to tape the conversation. Allbright argued that it hadn't been free consent because Anderson feared losing the immunity deal if he didn't agree to the body pack. Justice Maher considered the arguments but decided he wasn't persuaded that the immunity deal would have been lost if Anderson had refused. He said the tape could go into evidence.

The tape was played that afternoon for the jury. The sound was of excellent quality, although, because the rustle of Anderson's clothes sometimes obscured what was being said, the jurors were also issued transcripts of the conversation. Allbright hadn't wanted the jurors to have transcripts, feeling that this would influence the jury to give the tape more weight than other evidence.

Great precautions were taken to ensure that Anderson was not photographed, since he was to be relocated under a new identity. (The media, of course, regarded this as a challenge to their ingenuity.) The first day he testified, Anderson was brought into the courthouse lying down in the back seat of a car with a blanket over his head. The next morning the scenario was repeated. All but one of the photographers crowded the car and tried to shoot through the glass. The photographer who didn't was Jeff Vinnick, age twenty, from the Saskatoon *Star-Phoenix*. He had noticed the day before that the cardboard on one of the garage windows had fallen down, leaving about six inches of open space. Undetected by anyone, he walked up to the court window with a ladder. While Anderson was being driven in, and the police were occupied with the crowd of photographers around the car, Vinnick was silently taking pictures through the opening in the window. He managed to get two or three shots of Anderson getting out of the car without his blanket before he was ordered off the ladder by an angry RCMP officer.

Vinnick packed up his ladder and cameras and took off for his newspaper to make the afternoon deadline. The hometown photographer had managed to scoop the national media. He was also able to make a few dollars for himself by selling his pictures across the country.

That morning, October 23, Gerry Allbright came out swinging in his cross-examination. He asked Anderson if he believed in the commandment, "Thou shalt not kill," and Anderson replied: "Yes, I do."

"Thou shalt not kill, yourself, but it's okay to help someone else. Is that your personal interpretation?" Allbright queried.

For the rest of the day Allbright hammered at Anderson. What type of man, he asked, would do the things Anderson had done, for the money Thatcher gave him?

"I would say, someone who's a fool," Anderson replied.

Allbright accused Anderson of coming forward only because he knew the police regarded him as chief suspect in the murder.

"I believe they knew I had an involvement in it," Anderson replied. He added that he came forward because what he had done was wrong, not because he thought he was going to be charged.

"I believed that I had done wrong . . . knew that I had done wrong. Certainly the fact that I would be charged entered into it," he told the jury.

Allbright said there were two possible explanations for Anderson's appearance at the trial and his evidence. The first was that Anderson was a fool. The second, that he was lying. "With nothing to lose and perhaps $50,000 to gain you were prepared to say you were involved with something you didn't do," Allbright accused.

The jury were told about the $50,000 reward for information leading to the arrest and conviction of JoAnn Wilson's murderer.

Allbright then started in on Anderson's participation in getting the tape. He said Anderson's hyperventilating and nervousness weren't because he feared for his safety; instead they were "because you were walking the most important tightrope of your life. You had told the police the story you have given us yesterday and you'd led them to believe Colin Thatcher was involved in the murder of JoAnn Wilson.'' Allbright went on to point out that nowhere in the tape was there an unequivocal admission of wrongdoing by Colin Thatcher. Anderson replied that he hadn't wanted to spook Thatcher by being too specific, although the entire purpose of the tape was to try and gain a confession.

Allbright said that there had been plenty of opportunities for Anderson to say, ''I'm glad you killed her,'' or, ''I'm glad you killed JoAnn Wilson,'' but that Anderson ''did not do it because if you did, you would have gotten a genuine denial from Colin Thatcher.'' Such a remark, he added, would have brought ''an astonished look on his face and he would have said, 'What in the world are you talking about, Gary Anderson?' ''

''Why not put the nail in a little more? Why not use that phraseology?'' Allbright continued. ''You didn't do it because you know it is not true. He did not kill his wife. You did not put a nail in the coffin.''

Anderson admitted that he had lied to Thatcher in a couple of places on the tape, the most important lie being the comment about having a bitch of a time getting the blood off. ''I didn't try to get any blood off,'' he told the jury.

Anderson also admitted he had lied about being on holidays and about the ease with which a government job contract could be cancelled.

''Where you thought it suited your purpose on this tape you were prepared to lie, Mr. Anderson,'' Allbright said, adding, ''May I suggest you don't use the word 'murder' because you're going to get a genuine denial from Mr. Thatcher and that's not going to look good on your tape?

''If what you tell us is true, then [in] the mission you

set out to accomplish that morning in May . . . you failed miserably,'' Allbright finished.

Counsel for the defence then moved on to the question of the silencers for the gun. He wanted to know why Anderson was only able to provide the police with one of them and not the six he claimed had been made.

He also wanted to know how a silencer could be made when it required precision fitting. He wondered whether Doyle had been concerned that he was doing something illegal. He found it strange, Allbright continued, that Anderson had returned the gun holster to Thatcher, and wanted to know how Anderson had carried the illegal gun around.

''There may be safer ways, but I usually carried it wrapped in a rag,'' Anderson replied.

The defence lawyer then asked him about his convictions for pointing a firearm and the two assault-causing-bodily-harm charges, and questioned Anderson's assertion that Thatcher had been ''stalking'' JoAnn Wilson the week of the murder. ''Don't you find it strange he was stalking his wife when he could see her house from where he works [at the Legislative Building]?'' Allbright wanted to know.

The lawyer also asked why Anderson had waited until Sunday to pick up his car if he had loaned it to Thatcher for the murder. ''You've just loaned a car to a man to commit a killing and you hear about the killing and you don't rush out to pick the car up?'' Allbright said, registering some incredulity.

Last, but not least, Allbright asked, ''If for $1,000 to $1,200 lousy dollars . . . you'd participate in the taking of a human life, what would you do for $50,000? I suggest you would concoct a story to frame this man, Colin Thatcher,'' he added, in answer to his own question.

Anderson admitted that one reason he didn't take

the $50,000 to kill Wilson was because he didn't like the payment plan. "And also because I'm not a killer," he said.

Allbright then took the opportunity to say, referring to the reward money, "If Colin Thatcher is convicted by this good jury of the charge which he faces, you, Mr. Anderson, above all else, are the prime recipient for a share of that $50,000."

Allbright reminded the jurors that Anderson had turned on his own benefactors when he turned on the police, and suggested that the witness was an emotionally unstable man who could become violent.

When Allbright finally sat down, Anderson was very, very tired. It had been a long and intense day. Under re-examination he told the jury why he had come to testify. "I came here for one reason and that was to tell the truth as I understand it, the whole truth and nothing but the truth."

Kujawa pointed out to the jury, in re-examining Anderson, that the immunity from prosecution was only good if Anderson told the truth and had not participated in the actual killing of JoAnn.

Kujawa also asked the witness what the nature of the relationship was between Anderson and Thatcher.

"I don't travel with him, I don't go to parties. I just know him from the land. Other than the involvement with JoAnn Wilson, I have nothing else to do with him," was Anderson's response.

That night, Thatcher's minister, Ray Matheson from the Regina Bible College, went to visit him. Thatcher had become a Christian since his arrest and Matheson's visits to him in jail totalled about twenty.

Thatcher was greeted every morning by four or five photographers and television crews in their daily pursuit of fresh pictures and tapes. The press tried for three weeks to get Thatcher to say something on tape. One morning a reporter asked: "Can you say a few words about how you think things are going, Mr. Thatcher?''

"You guys probably wouldn't get it correct, anyway," Thatcher shot back.

Another morning, when it was −26°C, Thatcher walked out in his handcuffs, looked at the journalists and said, "It's too cold to fuck around this morning." Thatcher knew quotes like that would never be used.

The last day of the prosecution was devoted to the tying up of loose ends and to the evidence of Charlie Wilde. That morning the jury heard how Constables James McKee and Raymond Golemba of the Special Weapons and Tactics unit had kept surveillance on Anderson and Thatcher in the field. RCMP Constable Robert Britton described his aerial surveillance of the area, and RCMP Corporal Fred Waeltz described his ground surveillance of Thatcher's truck. Sergeant Jim Street took the stand to describe a trial run he had made from the scene of the murder to Colin Thatcher's home in Moose Jaw. It took, Street reported, twenty-eight minutes and nineteen seconds to drive the seventy-two kilometre (forty-five mile) distance in a police car. Thatcher, who appeared relaxed that morning, shook his head and chuckled while Allbright cross-examined Street.

Street had included forty-nine seconds for parking several blocks from the Moose Jaw house and running to the back door. He hit speeds of up to 175 km/hr on the trip.

Street rejected Allbright's suggestion that he would have had to drive 200 km/hr to cover the distance in that time. Allbright asked whether Street had had any trouble running in the snow or if he had simulated running with a gun or a weapon under his coat. The officer replied that there was no snow on the ground and that he hadn't pretended he was carrying anything.

Charlie Wilde was the last scheduled witness for the

Crown. He described his involvement with Thatcher and Anderson from November 1980 to the spring of 1981, when he had gone to jail again. The jury also heard about Wilde's ten-year hard drug habit. Allbright repeatedly asked him about it in cross-examination.

"It didn't fry your mind, witness, at all?" the lawyer wanted to know.

Wilde replied that he didn't think so, but admitted that drugs had gotten him into a lot of trouble over the years.

Thatcher's lawyer suggested that Wilde and his lawyer had persuaded the authorities to guarantee Wilde immunity from prosecution in the Wilson murder in return for his testimony. But Wilde replied: "They haven't discussed it with me."

Charlie also denied that he would be prepared to lie to get a slice of the $50,000 reward for the conviction of JoAnn's killer. "I'm not playing a role for money now," he said. "I guess that's the difference."

In total, twenty-seven witnesses had testified in person for the prosecution of Colin Thatcher for first-degree murder. A further witness's evidence had been accepted through an affidavit.

Although Kujawa closed his case that day, it wasn't to be the final word from the people's side. The Crown always has a chance to introduce reply evidence, and its final witness would be a surprise to everyone — but especially to Colin Thatcher.

CHAPTER THIRTEEN

The Defence

Gerry Allbright opened Thatcher's defence on Thursday, October 25, 1984, at 10 a.m.

The spectators in the court were eagerly awaiting Allbright's opening, hoping for clues to the defence strategy. But Allbright kept his cards close to his chest and gave nothing away.

"I have a number of witnesses to call who will have some interesting and informative evidence for the jury," Allbright said. That was the extent of his opening. The spectators were disappointed at the brevity of his message, although their curiosity was certainly heightened.

Allbright's first witness was Regina television reporter Wayne Mantyka. Mantyka had been served with two subpoenas to appear. He had received one, which was apparently unofficial, on Tuesday, while Allbright delivered the official one with the seal on Wednesday.

By calling Mantyka first, Allbright showed a certain amount of professional courtesy. Witnesses were excluded from the courtroom during the testimony of other witnesses for the same side. If Mantyka hadn't been called first thing in the morning, he would have had to wait his turn outside the courtroom, unable to cover the story.

Mantyka's evidence did not take long. He described how he had gone to the Saskatoon Gun Shop with his television crew and been able to purchase a box of .357 special, hollow-point, silver-tipped, plus-P bullets. During the same visit the shopkeeper showed him a hand-gun that the store stocked. Mantyka also placed an order for that particular type of bullet with an aluminum jacket. The aluminum jacket on the bullet is quite rare.

During cross-examination, Kujawa gave the witness a rougher time than anyone expected. Mantyka testified that he had concluded, on the basis of the evidence he'd heard, that the bullets were allowed in Canada for use with a shotgun or rifle. Kujawa crisply informed him that the bullets were only legal when fired from a .22-calibre rifle.

"I hope the jury is paying more attention to the evidence than you are," Kujawa told the reporter.

Mantyka later commented that at least Kujawa's toughness showed Mantyka was no set-up witness, but someone to be taken seriously.

When Mantyka left the stand, he resumed taking notes in the front row of the courtroom.

Allbright's next witness was Tony Merchant, Thatcher's divorce counsel and friend. Merchant, a well-known lawyer and Liberal, was a familiar face to many Saskatchewan residents. Allbright painstakingly took Merchant through his credentials in minute detail. After ten minutes devoted to Merchant's life history, it was clear that Allbright was going overboard in an effort to present Merchant as an upstanding citizen, in contrast to the less-than-savoury witnesses who had testified for the Crown.

Merchant had known Thatcher for more than twenty-five years. Initially, Merchant simply knew Colin as the premier's son. The pair became reacquainted in the early 1970s when Merchant was a Liberal MLA from 1975 to 1978, while Colin represented the Thunder Creek riding.

About a week after JoAnn left Colin, in August 1979, Merchant became involved. He stayed on the case until the bitter end. He admitted on the stand

184

that he was more than just a lawyer to Colin. He was a friend, too.

Merchant first gave evidence about the night of May 17, 1981, when the first shooting of JoAnn occurred. Merchant and his wife live less than 200 yards along the back alley from the home that JoAnn shared with Tony Wilson. On that night, the couple had gone to bed early. Allbright made sure the jury knew Merchant had spent the weekend as a supervisor at a cub scout camp.

Merchant couldn't put an exact time on when he was notified of the shooting. He had gone to bed about 8:15 p.m. Some time later, the nanny roused them from sleep to say that the police were at the door. The police then told Merchant that JoAnn had been shot and asked if Thatcher was at his home.

''I immediately called Mr. Thatcher,'' Merchant testified. He had direct-dialled the number of the Thatcher home in Moose Jaw, some seventy-two kilometres away. Regan Thatcher answered the phone and said that his father wasn't home. The boy later testified that he was told to say that because Colin was cleaning out the swimming pool.

Merchant insisted it was urgent, whereupon Colin came to the phone.

''I assumed the police would want to question him,'' Merchant testified. ''I wanted to tell him not to say anything until I was present.''

Merchant told the jury he had immediately dressed and left for Moose Jaw, often travelling at speeds over ninety miles an hour. The trip took him about thirty-five minutes from door to door. As he wheeled onto Redland Avenue, he could see that police cars had the Thatcher home staked out. Merchant went into the house, assuming it would be only a matter of minutes until the police came to the door. He and Thatcher sat for some time while Merchant advised Colin what to say when the officers arrived. To their surprise, how-

185

ever, the police never approached the door. Merchant left some hours later.

There were large discrepancies among Regan's, Merchant's and Thatcher's evidence about the time of the phone call that night. Merchant couldn't place an exact time on it, Regan thought it happened early in the evening and Thatcher testified that it came around 11 p.m. and that it was Greg who called him to the phone, not Regan.

The exact time of the shooting was never released until that day in court. Kujawa asked Merchant on cross-examination if he would disagree that he could have arrived at the Redland Avenue house at 12:45 a.m. The question seemed to surprise Merchant, but because he knew the police had watched him pull into the Thatcher driveway, he didn't argue.

Merchant was even more surprised when Kujawa informed him that the shooting had happened at exactly 10:10 p.m. If Merchant called Thatcher thirty-five minutes before 12:45, the call would have been made around midnight. Merchant's telephone records confirm that the call was made between the twenty-third and twenty-fourth hours of the day. If the shooting occurred at 10:10 p.m., Thatcher would have had ample time to drive the seventy-two kilometres back to Moose Jaw.

Kujawa also pointed out that Merchant could have been charged with dangerous driving. He wanted to know why Merchant was so desperate to get out to Moose Jaw if Thatcher hadn't done anything wrong.

"I wanted him not to answer any questions except in my presence," Merchant said. The lawyer told the jury he believed it was a good practice not to submit to police questioning before getting legal advice.

Merchant next gave evidence about the night of the murder. On January 21, 1983, around 6:10 or 6:15 p.m., Merchant learned that there were a lot of police cars around the Wilson home, and that it appeared there had been another shooting there.

He testified that again he immediately phoned Thatcher in Moose Jaw and told him what had happened. "You've got to be kidding," was Thatcher's reaction.

Merchant said he couldn't confirm the seriousness of the shooting until some time after 7 p.m., when he phoned Thatcher again to tell him JoAnn was dead.

Once again, in cross-examination Kujawa took exception to Merchant's times. The Crown wanted to know why Merchant's original affidavit in one of the bail hearings stated that he thought the call took place around 6:30 p.m. Existing telephone records revealed only the hour of the call, not the precise time. Merchant could give no explanation for the difference in times.

At one point Merchant told the jury he had no idea the police believed Thatcher was responsible for JoAnn's murder until he heard it in a bail application.

Merchant was also asked to explain the sequence of events that had led to the mischief and abduction charges against him and Thatcher. He said he had consulted with one of his partners and later came to believe that Tony Wilson would have no interest in keeping Stephanie after her mother's death.

Thatcher went to the Wilson home the day after the murder. Just after noon, he turned up at Merchant's door, visibly upset. He told his lawyer that he had found out that Stephanie was playing at a neighbour's, and asked Merchant to come with him.

During the examination-in-chief Merchant called what followed an "incident". However, when Kujawa started his cross-examination it became apparent that it was more than an incident.

Merchant said he couldn't recall that the scene was a bad one. He and Thatcher had opened the door and shouted into the house. The neighbour, Susan Kohli, had invited them in, he said. Merchant did not recollect that Kohli, a slight woman, had pulled at Thatcher's pants to try and stop him from taking the child. He said he "didn't believe" that any harsh words had been exchanged.

Kujawa didn't press Merchant on his recollection of the scene. He did ask if Merchant thought the Thatcher divorce was "extremely bitter". Merchant replied that all divorces were bitter and that this one was really no different from the rest. Kujawa wanted to know how Merchant felt about the remarks Mr. Justice Ted Noble had made about his part in the contempt proceedings against Thatcher. Noble had called Merchant's tactics "highly improper" and "an affront to the court". Merchant said he didn't think the remarks were that bad.

Before he left the stand, Merchant took a shot at the Regina police force. He testified that the original copies of the phone bill detailing his calls to Thatcher on the nights of the shootings had been paperclipped to the outside of Merchant's files on the Thatcher case. The files, which were kept in Merchant's office, had mysteriously disappeared during a break-in in which, Merchant added, no money or liquor was taken.

"I believe there would have been benefit to the police in their investigation to look in my files," Merchant testified.

Kujawa wanted to know just how far Merchant would go in his friendship for Thatcher. He pointed out that Thatcher gave Merchant's law firm a great deal of business, including some from the Saskatchewan government. (That is believed to be one of the reasons for Thatcher's ouster from the cabinet. Many good Conservatives thought the business should go to Tory lawyers rather than to a Liberal law firm.)

Merchant left the stand after more than half a day of testimony. It was unclear whether he had made any real gains for Thatcher.

Allbright next called Barbara Wright, twenty-seven, the wife of one of Thatcher's ranch employees. The couple live in a house on the ranch.

She testified that she had arrived home from work at about 4:35 p.m. on the day of the murder and, at about 5 p.m., started to make supper. She was sure of the times because she always leaves her job as a physiotherapist in Moose Jaw at 4:15 p.m. and spends about twenty minutes travelling the fifteen miles of highway from Moose Jaw to the Thatcher ranch on the south side of Caron.

"I had already started making supper. . . . Colin drove into the yard and got out and started checking cattle," Wright testified. She said the rancher stayed at least twenty minutes and left the ranch between 5:20 and 5:30 p.m.

Shortly after, her husband came in, and while Wright was cutting his hair the phone rang. "Colin called to say someone had murdered JoAnn," Wright recalled. She said Colin's reaction was "shock".

Later the police brought a picture of a suspect to the hospital where she worked and asked if she'd seen that man around Caron. She replied that she hadn't.

On cross-examination, Kujawa wanted to know why her hospital record for January 21, 1983, showed that she wasn't working that day.

"The hospital record is wrong," Wright said. She explained that she had changed shifts with someone but hadn't changed the schedule.

On March 7, 1983, two detectives visited Wright in her home. Kujawa said that she had told them she hadn't seen Thatcher for months. Wright denied making any such statement. During the trial, her husband was still working for Thatcher and the pair still lived on his ranch.

The next witness to trudge to the stand in defence of Colin Thatcher was twenty-four-year-old Pat Hammond, the brother of Sandra Silversides, the housekeeper the Thatchers still employ.

Hammond, a brakeman from CPR and a part-time mechanic, had come in from Moose Jaw the night before he testified. He, like nearly all of the witnesses, stayed at the Ramada Renaissance and relaxed on the night before his ordeal with several drinks and a whirlpool. When Greg Thatcher found Hammond talking to one of the journalists in the poolside bar that evening, he whispered to Hammond to ''be careful'' and not discuss the evidence any more. At least one journalist knew in detail, hours before Hammond appeared, the evidence that he would give.

Hammond testified that his parents lived about three blocks from the Thatcher home and that he'd known the family for about eight years. During this time, he'd done a fair amount of bodywork and mechanical repairs on the Thatcher vehicles and knew the Thatchers quite well.

He told the jury that he had seen Thatcher in Moose Jaw at about 5:30 p.m. on the day of the murder.

''I seen him at the corner of Saskatchewan and Redland at 5:30, very close to 5:30, within five minutes, anyway,'' Hammond testified.

Hammond said he knew without a doubt that it was Thatcher because he recognized the distinctive brown-and-neutral GMC four-by-four truck with the mobile-telephone antenna. Hammond told the jury he knew the exact time because he had been shopping in a store that closed at 5:30 p.m. and that the doors had been locked behind him when he left.

During cross-examination, Kujawa produced a signed affidavit in which Hammond said he saw Thatcher ''between 5 and 5:30 p.m.'' on that day.

''I guess I should have been more accurate on the affidavit,'' Hammond replied feebly. Kujawa also wanted to know why Hammond called JoAnn a few "nasty names" when the police visited him on February 11, 1983.

"I did not like the woman," Hammond replied.

After Hammond left the stand, Allbright stood up and asked if he could re-examine the witness. Justice Maher refused. "You examined in chief and pinned him down to . . . after 5:30 because the store closed at 5:30, and he said positively . . . I know the store closed at 5:30 and I left so it must have been after 5:30. Now Mr. Kujawa discredits that evidence by an affidavit. Isn't that the end of it? Isn't it up to the jury now?" the judge finished.

"Well, that's my lord's choice of words, discredit," Allbright replied.

Sandra Silversides was the next witness to testify. The blonde woman came across as shy, soft-spoken and demure for the first half of her testimony. But when cross-examination started, another side of Sandra began to emerge, revealing the twenty-two-year-old who was perfectly capable of efficiently running her own household and the Thatcher household, while holding both a full-time job and a part-time job as Thatcher's constituency secretary, a combination of jobs that brought in close to $40,000 a year.

She told the jury that January 21, 1983, was her day off work. She stayed at home until about 5 p.m. and then walked over to the Thatcher home.

She saw Greg and Regan in the house and went to the kitchen to start making Hamburger Helper. Silversides testified that sometime before 6 p.m., while she was in the kitchen, Thatcher came in.

The hamburger was ready right about 6 p.m., and the family sat down to eat. Being quick eaters, they had finished dinner by about 6:10 p.m.

"I just told them it was their turn to clean up and I went home," Silversides told the court.

About an hour later, while she was in the bathtub,

Greg phoned her at home and told her that something had happened to his mother. Silversides dressed and went back to the house.

"I really didn't know what to do," she said. She started to call members of Thatcher's political executive to give them the news.

"He was just sitting at the kitchen table, staring at the wall," she recalled.

There was nothing she could do for Thatcher so she busied herself with the boys. "Regan was very subdued and didn't want to talk about it," she remembered.

Allbright asked her next about the day Thatcher was arrested. When she heard the news she reported, "I just about passed out."

About an hour after she had learned of Thatcher's arrest, Silversides said, two policemen came to her door and told her she'd be arrested. While she related this part of the story in court, her eyes filled with tears and her lower lip began to tremble.

"They took all my jewellery and my purse and I was fingerprinted and pictures were taken. I started to cry," she testified.

Silversides was told she was going to be charged with accessory to murder, before and after the fact, but was later released and not charged. "The only reason I was at the Thatchers' was to take care of the children," she said.

Kujawa had some questions for Silversides in cross-examination. One matter that concerned him was the $10,500 in cheques, written by Thatcher, deposited in her account over a period of three months in 1980–81. There was a cheque in November 1980 for $1,500, another $1,500 cheque in December, a $1,500 cheque in January 1981 and a $1,000 cheque in February. Also in February there was a deposit for $3,000 and a $2,200 withdrawal. Silversides testified that her salary from Thatcher for housekeeping duties was only $500 a month. She said other cheques were to reimburse her for money spent initially out of her own pocket to keep the Thatcher household running.

Kujawa also asked her about her pending lawsuit against the Regina City Police for her arrest and imprisonment. Silversides' former boyfriend, Blaine Matheson, had given a statement to the police in which he said that Silversides had once told him there was a Mustang in the garage with a rifle in it. She denied ever saying that. The lawsuit had been postponed pending the results of the criminal trial and was set to start again.

Kujawa had one last trick in his bag for Sandra.

She had said she was in the kitchen between 5 and 6 p.m. on January 21, preparing dinner. He said she was on the phone for most of that time talking to her ex-boyfriend.

"Well, I don't remember," she replied.

Kujawa jogged her memory, reminding her that the call had lasted from 5:32 to 5:58 p.m. Silversides stopped for a second and then looked shocked.

"You don't want me to say his name, do you?" Kujawa asked her.

"Well, I made a lot of phone calls," she replied lamely.

On the morning of the next day of the trial, Friday, October 26, Thatcher's sons took the stand to testify on their father's behalf. The testimony of the two teenagers made a total of six people who placed Thatcher in Moose Jaw at the time of the killing.

The boys' evidence was similar. They both testified that the Hamburger Helper was made just before 6 p.m., and that their father had joined them for dinner.

Regan confirmed that he had answered the phone the night of the first shooting and had called to his father, who was cleaning the pool at the time. Greg said that he was home at the time, as well.

Greg told the jury that he didn't remember Sandra making a telephone call the evening of his mother's death but that possibly she did. He emphatically denied that Sandra ever encouraged him and his brother to call JoAnn "the bitch".

"She never said anything bad about mother," Greg said. Regan echoed that in his testimony.

The boys finished giving evidence by about 11:30 a.m. Allbright stood and told the judge the defence had moved much quicker than he'd anticipated and that he would prefer to start fresh on Monday with a "very, very major witness". Justice Maher agreed, and court was adjourned for the day.

Allbright was mobbed outside by reporters who wanted to know if Colin was going to testify. Allbright refused to comment, but winked broadly at them. Speculation continued over the weekend about the major witness and, sure enough, on Monday, October 29, Colin Thatcher took the stand in his own defence. Thatcher risked damage to himself by taking the stand, because he would have to submit to Kujawa's unrelenting cross-examination.

Many theories about why Allbright would allow Thatcher to take the stand were advanced. Some people believed that Thatcher, in his usual arrogant manner, had simply told Allbright he wanted to testify and that he wouldn't give up until Allbright agreed.

And he was a politician. Reporters who'd seen him in action in the Legislature likened his performance at his murder trial to his style in the House. "It was like the old Thatcher," one reporter said. "That's exactly the way he used to talk in the House to his opponents."

Thatcher sailed through his examination-in-chief. He told the jury how hard he had tried to be a good husband, and how shattered he had been when the marriage crumbled. He never referred to the fact that he had committed adultery during his marriage.

He said that the problems had started when JoAnn "changed" just before she turned forty, after which she went out and had an affair with his best friend.

"JoAnn and I had an excellent marriage. . . . We had the same trivial disagreements as everyone else, but we had an excellent marriage," he declared.

Thatcher told the court that his wife was a troubled and unhappy person whom he couldn't help, and that he had wanted a reconciliation for a long time after the marriage break-up.

The rancher described the lengths he went to get his children back from JoAnn when she first left. On one occasion, he flew down to Ames, Iowa, to see the Geigers and look for JoAnn there. Later he flew to Brampton with Sandra and brought Stephanie and Regan back with him.

Thatcher also gave an account of his Christmas 1979 visit to Dick Collver's ranch in Arizona, during which the two men had a drunken discussion of Thatcher's options in the divorce trial.

"Dick is the cheapest drunk in the world," Thatcher said." Dick has no capacity for alcohol and that is why he rarely drinks." He then reported what Collver had said when he was half drunk and half hungover: "You can be bled to death financially, you can settle the matter before the lawyers get to it or you can kill her," he said Collver had told him.

"It was an unacceptable option," Thatcher said of Collver's suggestion.

The politician added that he had decided of his own volition to leave the Collver ranch — that he and his family were not asked to leave.

Thatcher also explained why Regan had refused to stay with his mother: "Regan had become very turned off by his mother during his trip to Texas [with JoAnn and Ron Graham]. He said to me, 'You know, Dad, she thought I didn't know what was going on when

195

they closed the door. I know everything.' He was nine years old when he said that.''

When Regan refused to go with JoAnn, despite the court order, Thatcher dismissed his own contempt of court by saying to the jury that he had had no option but to send the child away.

''It was a terrible option,'' he commented.

The financial settlement with the Wilsons was made simply because they were ''sick of lawyers, sick of courts and sick of being bled financially''. He made no reference to the conversations he and Wilson had had.

Thatcher denied any involvement with the shooting of JoAnn in May 1981, and said that he was at home cleaning the swimming pool when it occurred.

After the shooting in which JoAnn was wounded, Thatcher received the seven roses and went out and bought his gun. ''I was overreacting to the roses by buying a gun. . . . At the same time I was conjuring up all kinds of images of having to use that gun,'' he said.

Thatcher's explanation for the missing gun was that the cleaning lady likely took it while he was in Canada. He denied ever packing it in a box and smuggling it back to Moose Jaw. ''Rightly or wrongly, I came to the conclusion that the cleaning lady had taken it. I changed cleaning ladies after.''

He also described his ''feeling of sickness'' on hearing that JoAnn had been murdered, and vehemently denied any involvement. In fact, he was not in Regina at all the week of the killing, because he was home licking his ''political wounds'' after being bounced from the cabinet. He refused to say why he was bounced, because of his vow of cabinet secrecy. ''It had been one blazes of a tough week,'' he summed up the week his ex-wife was killed.

Thatcher dismissed large portions of Lynne Mendell's evidence, saying that her recollection was faulty, insisting that he and Mendell had parted on good terms, and admitting that he was "disappointed" when she testified against him at the preliminary hearing.

There were times he had cared for Lynne, he said, but he had never really trusted her. He made a point of the fact that he wouldn't allow her to drive his $40,000 Mercedes in Palm Springs because he didn't have enough confidence in her. It seemed a strange comment from a man who had entrusted Lynne with the care of his children.

The relationship had been stormy, he conceded, largely because Lynne was unstable. He pointed to her suicide attempt and the pregnancy alarm as proof of that. He also denied that he had ever confessed to her, or said to her that he had wounded his wife.

The night of JoAnn's murder, Thatcher reported, Lynne had reacted with genuine shock and surprise. "There was no question she was concerned," he said. His version of the conversation he and Lynne had had about JoAnn's murder was as follows: "We were in bed and she asked me quietly, 'Did you blow her away?' I said, 'I cannot imagine what a strange feeling that would be. Of course not.' "

By the spring of that year, the relationship was over, but they had reached a point where they could meet for drinks occasionally. Lynne even set up a blind date for Colin once.

Lynne had learned of the beating during the murder from press clippings that Canadian guests had sent to her parents in Palm Springs. Thatcher denied telling Mendell he didn't beat JoAnn. "I said: 'Whoever was in there was an animal anyway. No one could do that to another person,' " he reported.

After Thatcher had testified about Mendell, court adjourned for the day. His explanation of Gary Anderson's testimony was to follow on Tuesday. The already enormous public interest in the trial intensified

197

further when Thatcher took the stand. The public started lining up for seats at 2 a.m. despite the − 20°C temperatures. At one point, when two women had a loud argument on the courthouse steps, the Saskatoon City Police had to be called in to patrol the lines during the lunch break. Tempers flared periodically as people jealously guarded their spots in line.

Tuesday morning, Thatcher took the stand again and spun a story that explained Anderson's descriptions of their meetings.

He said that because Anderson was an unsavoury character, he had wanted to stay on his good side. Anderson, Thatcher said, had approached him for the first time in early 1981, informing Thatcher that he had a friend who could help Thatcher "do a number" on Ron Graham's construction business because he knew Graham was cutting corners. Thatcher said he agreed to meet Anderson and the friend and pay Anderson's expenses. The pair then put forward a harebrained scheme, which involved setting Graham up with a girl, or laying a "good licking" on him. They also, Thatcher said, offered to beat JoAnn up.

Thatcher claimed that he sent them on their way. A few days later Anderson resurfaced and asked for $500 for expenses because he had car trouble. Thatcher said the man with Anderson that day did not look like Charlie Wilde but he couldn't be sure.

Thatcher didn't see Anderson again until 1982, when he reported a blackmail incident to Anderson. A man had phoned Thatcher and said not only that he knew Gary Anderson, but also that he knew the details of Thatcher's conversation with Anderson, and was going to cause trouble.

Thatcher told the jury he didn't see Anderson again until the fall of 1982 when Anderson approached him in the parking lot outside the Legislature.

During Thatcher's testimony, the jurors, who had

till then been extraordinarily attentive to the evidence, began to look bored, shifting uncomfortably in their seats and looking impatient as he talked. At the Legislature, he said, Anderson invited Thatcher to get into a brown car, an early '70s model, that had just then pulled up nearby. Thatcher climbed in and laid his topcoat and gloves on the seat.

Anderson said he needed Thatcher's assistance. He had left a car in the parking lot and it had been towed away. Thatcher said he agreed to make enquiries and got out of the car, forgetting his belongings in the back seat.

Colin denied that any of the meetings at the time of the shooting, the murder or the gun transfer had occurred. He told the jury that the next time he saw Anderson was the day the tape was recorded, May 1, 1984.

He said he knew rumours were rampant that the police were suggesting he had hired Anderson to kill JoAnn and that he had gotten Anderson a government job — an explanation that would cover the remarks Thatcher had made on the tape about the police tying the pair together.

Thatcher had an explanation for everything. The remarks about the gun and the blood, he said, were Gary Anderson's idea of a "sick joke". When Anderson said, "I'm glad you got her," he was referring to the custody of Stephanie, not the murder of JoAnn. When Anderson spoke of "getting rid" of the stuff in the car, Thatcher said he was talking about the topcoat and gloves. And the famous "deny, deny, deny" remark he dismissed with the comment, "If you haven't done anything wrong, then of course you should deny it."

Anderson's motive for lying and setting Thatcher up was, of course, money. "Of course you've got the spectre of the $50,000 reward. . . . It's always been one of my theories that for $50,000 they can probably buy a witness."

After lunch that day, Kujawa stood up to start what turned into a sharp and sizzling cross-examination. It was the most riveting afternoon of the trial.

The encounter between accused and prosecutor was like a street brawl. Kujawa dragged Thatcher quickly from point to point, firing sharp questions at him and knocking his testimony down at every step.

He began with Thatcher's trip to Palm Springs with Ron Graham. "I suggest to you that you were 'doing' one Janice Gardiner while you were golfing in between," he said.

Thatcher was cornered. He had to admit the adultery because it had been proved in divorce court. He also admitted to having a different set of girls on the previous trip with Graham.

Kujawa asked him about cruelty to JoAnn. Thatcher denied he'd ever laid a hand on her and asserted that she received her black eyes when he accidentally struck her while falling from a ladder. This was a completely different story from the one in Thatcher's divorce affidavit, in which he said he had rolled over in bed and struck JoAnn's nose by mistake.

Kujawa accused Thatcher of being the type of person who always blamed someone else for his problems. Why, he asked, were three or four different banks suing Thatcher? And was it not convenient for the politician that JoAnn's death set back the divorce settlement payment schedule by a year? He also forced Thatcher to admit that he had absolutely no explanation for how his credit-card slip wound up only metres from Wilson's body.

Kujawa pushed harder, asking how Thatcher had managed to get all the witnesses to testify for him, whereupon Thatcher exploded at the implication that his sons were lying.

He lurched forward in the witness box, half lifting himself out of the seat, and gave a demonstration of the famous — and feared — Thatcher temper. Many of those in the courtroom felt afraid just watching a few seconds of it, even in that protected environment.

"Then if you think they did not tell the truth why don't you do something about it?" he yelled. "It's very easy to say my sons have lied. Why don't you step out on the courthouse steps and say that?"

"Charlie Bronson, you're not," Kujawa coolly replied.

The defendant's temper flashed again a few minutes later when the subject of his bail applications came up. Thatcher said staying in jail in Regina was like living in hell. He lurched forward again and glared intensely at Kujawa, claiming that Kujawa had grossly misrepresented the tape at the bail hearing by saying there were threats to at least three people on it.

"And because of that gross misrepresentation, I spent six months in jail," he yelled. "And I categorically deny there were threats and a confession. I've spent six months in jail because of it," he shouted furiously.

Any doubters who may have thought reports of Colin Thatcher's temper were exaggerated doubted no longer. He'd shown himself to be a volatile man who couldn't keep his temper at his own murder trial.

The outbursts did a great deal of damage to his credibility. Kujawa swiftly drove that point home. "I suggest to you that your wife lived in great fear of you — physical fear," Kujawa said. He followed up a few questions later with: "During those arguments did you talk to her the way you just talked to me?" adding, "I suggest to you that when you get mad, you get wild."

"I don't think that was getting wild," Thatcher replied.

Perhaps most damaging to his credibility was his

invitation to Kujawa to step outside. Was Thatcher implying that Kujawa was trading on his courtroom immunity to make remarks that would otherwise have netted him a slander suit? Or did the remark mean that Thatcher wanted to settle the argument with his fists?

Allbright had precious little re-examination. He asked Thatcher to clarify what he meant by the invitation to Kujawa. Thatcher replied that he wanted Serge to make the comments where he could be sued for them.

Perhaps the most important part of the cross-examination of Thatcher was in relation to the tape. It provided an opportunity to present the Crown's view in a dramatic manner. The tape had to be viewed in the light of the other evidence and it had to be studied in great detail. The purpose of the cross-examination was mainly to explain over and over how each line fitted one view of the case and not another. It allowed for the playing of key parts of the conversation and for showing that Thatcher could not give an acceptable explanation. Almost a whole day was spent on the cross-examination in relation to the tape. This opportunity for the Crown to present its argument so fully through the cross-examination made it questionable whether Thatcher helped himself by testifying.

Having spent hours in presenting the final argument in this manner, Kujawa could well afford to be brief in his formal final summation.

Finally, Thatcher rejoined Allbright at the defence table. There were no more witnesses for the defence, Allbright said. It was Wednesday morning, October 31.

Kujawa then rose and asked Justice Maher if he could raise a matter in the absence of the jury. That matter was the evidence of Dick Collver and the Thatcher family's wretched Christmas visit to the Collver ranch.

The appearance of Dick Collver in Saskatoon was most opportune for the Crown's case. Collver and his wife, Eleanor, had recently travelled to Saskatoon from their home in Phoenix, Arizona, to be with their daughter for the birth of their grandchild. Collver had been spotted in the Ramada elevator during the trial, and Swayze decided to talk to him, while rumours that he might be called as a witness for the defence began to circulate. When Kujawa learned of Collver's presence, he invited Collver in for a talk — an invitation delivered by the police, who located Collver at the local YMCA where he was having a massage. He wanted to tell them what he had painfully hidden.

When the Crown and Collver met, Kujawa learned for the first time of that dreadful Christmas visit. Collver described in great detail Colin's obsession with JoAnn and consequent refusal to let the matter drop — an obsession that ultimately interfered with the long-standing friendship between the two politicians.

Thatcher sat shaking his head through most of Collver's testimony. Allbright asked Collver on cross-examination about a phone call he had made to Peggy Thatcher when he learned of Colin's arrest.

"You said, 'I'm terribly sorry to hear about it. Is there anything I can do to help?' Was this what you had in mind?" Allbright asked scathingly.

"I'm sorry, sir," Collver replied. "I meant, to help *her*."

Allbright grilled him about the legal advice he'd received as well as the length of time he'd waited to come forward with his story. Collver had contacted his lawyers three times to find out what his legal obligations were. Each time he was told he had none. Collver explained to the jury that he was reluctant to come forward because he wanted to save his family from further press attention. However, he now realized he had been wrong. He admitted he had for a while put his legal responsibility ahead of his moral responsibility.

"I have to say to you," Collver told Allbright, "instead of phoning Ron Barclay [Collver's lawyer] in 1979, if I'd phoned somebody else, another human being might be alive. Perhaps I was wrong."

Collver's testimony ended with a hint of sadness when Allbright asked him how he felt about Colin Thatcher.

"I consider him my friend today," Collver replied, glancing over at Thatcher sitting at the defence table.

"Would it surprise you to know he considers you one of his better friends?" Allbright asked.

"I think we both feel the same way," Collver replied gently.

After the jury left that day, Allbright said he might like to reopen his case to rebut Collver's evidence. Kujawa had no objections.

"If this evidence had been available earlier, we would have called it earlier," he said. "He [Allbright] is free to recall whatever witnesses he wants."

Allbright told the judge he'd likely recall Colin to the stand in the morning. In the end, however, Thatcher didn't make another appearance. He had already given his evidence of the visit and there was nothing more he could add.

The trial was drawing rapidly to a close. All that remained were the lawyers' addresses to the jury and the judge's charge.

Allbright went first, after lunch on November 1. His eighty-seven-minute address had flair and great dramatic effect.

He started by telling the jurors that the Canadian justice system was on trial right along with Colin Thatcher. Many people, he told them, didn't believe a fair trial was possible for the flashy politician.

"There's never been an accused where there's been

204

so much written and said about him. . . . I don't envy the twelve of you," said Allbright. "We have an unprecedented situation in this courtroom. . . . The twelve of you are making history."

He likened the trial to life itself — it was a case that encompassed tragedy, humour and drama. He also told the jurors that the true test of any justice system was its universality.

"Does it cover everyone? . . . This man sitting right here by me, Colin Thatcher, sits in this courtroom an innocent man."

If the jurors followed their consciences, Allbright asserted, there was only one verdict they could return — a verdict of "not guilty." He listed five different pieces of evidence that exonerated Thatcher from the murder charge.

First, there was Dotson's evidence. Allbright reminded the jury that Dotson's description of the man leaving the garage did not resemble Colin Thatcher. Second, telephone records showed that Thatcher had placed a call to Palm Springs from his home in Moose Jaw at 6:24 p.m. on the night of the murder.

Third, in Thatcher's own statement on the tape, he asserted that he was at home in Moose Jaw with four people on the night of the slaying. Fourth, six witnesses had placed Thatcher in Moose Jaw. It would be impossible, said Allbright, to convince that many people to lie on one's behalf.

"How many people do you know that would lie on a first-degree murder charge?" he asked the jury.

The fifth piece of evidence was the credit-card slip.

"This tells you Colin Thatcher could not have been the killer," Allbright said. "Only an insane person would drop their own calling card. If I wanted to frame Colin Thatcher I would leave it. . . . It's neatly folded and it's lying on the ground."

The jury may have felt Allbright was reaching for

that point. The only explanation given for the slip was the rather vague one offered by Thatcher himself. He sometimes didn't lock the truck in Moose Jaw, he had said, so that it would have been possible for someone to reach into his glove compartment and remove the slip in order to frame him by leaving it at the murder scene.

Allbright then started to attack the Crown's case. He told the jury to consider why some witnesses weren't called: the two senior police officers on the case; Danny Doyle, the man who made the silencers; and Cody Crutcher. He wondered aloud where Gary Anderson's brother-in-law was, and added that Dick Collver was called only because the Crown saw its case "slipping away" and had to do something drastic to revive it.

He then tried to discredit several witnesses' testimony. Mendell, he said, was a woman who was "prepared to be intimate with a man who was a killer."

"Lynne Mendell didn't want to love Colin Thatcher, she didn't even have to like him. She just wanted to marry him. She's got the problem of Palm Springs time warp."

Charlie Wilde's evidence he dismissed because Wilde was a drug addict. Then Allbright turned to Gary Anderson.

The biggest failure in Anderson's life was the time he spent on the witness stand and the fact that he couldn't get a confession from Thatcher on the tape. "Are you going to convict Colin Thatcher of first-degree murder on what that witness said?" Allbright asked incredulously. "There isn't a shred of evidence—not a shred—that Colin Thatcher committed this offence."

For good measure, he appealed to the jurors' consciences. He reminded them how terrible it would be if they made a mistake. He mentioned Donald Marshall, the Nova Scotian Micmac Indian who had spent ten years in prison for a murder he didn't commit, and then brought up the matter of nurse Susan Nelles, who had gone through a preliminary hearing on charges of murdering four babies at the world-renowned Hospital for Sick Children in Toronto.

In conclusion, Allbright pointed out that, considering the climate of public opinion, it would certainly be *easy* to convict Colin Thatcher.

"But, I suggest to you, that doesn't require the personal conviction or the courage that a verdict of innocence does," he finished.

It was the afternoon break. The jury filed out of the room. And Kujawa rose slowly and deliberately to his feet. He mentioned nine points that he felt Allbright had no legal or ethical right to bring up before the jury.

Allbright's remark that Collver was only a last-ditch attempt to save a sinking case was improper, Kujawa argued. Moreover, Allbright knew that some witnesses hadn't been called because they weren't admissible in the trial, anyway. With some heat, the Crown also declared that Allbright had no right to bring up the Marshall or Nelles cases; such allusions would only upset the jury and intimidate them with the possibility of making a mistake. And he objected to Allbright's mention of the 6:24 p.m. phone call to Palm Springs, since there had been no direct evidence called during the trial to prove that point. Kujawa asked the judge to rectify all of those points before he started his own address.

Justice Maher considered the matter for about half an hour. The jury was recalled and he addressed them on two issues. The first was Allbright's reference to Dick Collver. The judge said that Collver wasn't called just "on a whim". "I considered the matter and came to the conclusion that it was in your best interest to hear the evidence," he told the jury. As for the additional witnesses that Kujawa never called, the judge told the jurors that it was unlikely those witnesses' evidence would have been admissible. He added that the Crown had the obligation to disclose all the facts and that the jurors' obligation was "to decide the evidence on what is here before you now."

The judge then nodded to Kujawa, who stood up to give his twenty-two-minute address.

Kujawa's delivery was simple and eloquent, his argument straightforward. He tried in his summing-up to boil the case down to its essentials, so as not to confuse people with extraneous detail.

"Most of us will tell the truth unless we have a strong motive to lie," he told the jury, and then referred them to Lynne Mendell's evidence. "No one was able to suggest a motive for why she lied," he said simply.

He also pointed out that her evidence was consistent. How could she possibly know that the police would find a doll box with a Los Angeles newspaper in Thatcher's bedroom? It's quite simple, he said. She didn't. And that made her story consistent.

Charlie Wilde's story was consistent, too, Kujawa said. There was no motive for him to lie. The testimonies all fitted together, despite the varying natures of Mendell, Wilde and Anderson.

Of the tape and Anderson's evidence, Kujawa said it was his "submission that the tape fits the rest of the evidence like a transparency which makes sense of the parts underneath." As far as Kujawa was concerned, the tape was "a complete, plain, ordinary English confession" by Thatcher. It was clear, he said, that the pair talked "about nothing but murder".

"I suggest to you, ladies and gentlemen, that on the evidence you have to find beyond a reasonable doubt . . . .You will have no difficulty. Twelve reasonable people will find that the accused, Colin Thatcher, likely killed his wife himself. But it doesn't exclude the possibility that he had it done. In either case, he is equally guilty," Kujawa said.

"I know it is an awesome responsibility," he continued. "I believe you have the courage to bring in the only verdict that the evidence will support. Guilty as charged." Then he sat down.

Court was over for the day. Just before the jury departed, the judge reminded them not to expose themselves to media reports. The following day the judge would give the jury his instructions.

Mr. Justice Maher's charge lasted ninety-five minutes. The judge carefully spelled out for the jury three different options: guilty of first-degree murder, guilty of second-degree murder or not guilty. However, just before he issued the second-degree option, Justice Maher told the jury: "If you find the accused did it or caused it to be done, I suggest the evidence is almost overwhelming that it is first-degree murder."

The judge reviewed all the evidence that had been placed before the jury, the testimony of thirty-six witnesses, plus thirty-four exhibits. A large portion of his address was directed towards the Crown's evidence.

The judge told the jurors that when they considered the credibility of Lynne Mendell's evidence they should ask themselves how she would know about a box and a newspaper in which Thatcher wrapped the .357 magnum to smuggle it back to Canada if she wasn't telling the truth.

Her evidence was backed up by the discovery the police had made when they searched the Thatcher home. The police found a similar box, containing a Los Angeles newspaper, in the closet of Thatcher's bedroom. Mendell would have had no way of knowing it was there.

The judge also pointed out that the bullet fragments

found in JoAnn's brain were consistent with the type of bullets Thatcher had bought in California. Although the murder weapon was never found, the testimony showed that Thatcher's .357 magnum could have been the gun used in the slaying.

The judge also instructed the jury to remember Mendell's testimony about the bitterness that Thatcher felt towards JoAnn. That evidence was strongly supported by the testimony of Gary Anderson and Dick Collver. He admitted that Charlie Wilde and Anderson weren't "the most desirable people in the world" with whom to associate, but pointed out that, when looking for a killer for your wife, the "local vicar or the parish priest" are unlikely to apply.

He then told the jury that the stories of Mendell, Anderson and Wilde tended to support each other.

On Charlie Wilde, he added that Wilde "claimed blatantly and shamelessly that he had ripped off Colin Thatcher." He observed that Wilde was hardly a man of exemplary character or "lofty moral persuasion" and urged the jury to approach the evidence of Wilde and Anderson with "care and caution." Nevertheless, if Thatcher was telling the truth and had never met Wilde, how did Wilde know that JoAnn's parents lived in Iowa, that her father was a professor and that Thatcher owned a Corvette?

As a further postscript to his remarks about Wilde, the judge said that he found Charlie's assertion that his drug use had not affected his brain "somewhat difficult to accept." "It does sound somewhat incredible that he has a brain," he admitted. But then he reminded the jurors that when Allbright asked Wilde why he didn't continue to blackmail Thatcher, Wilde replied, "You do not go back to the well too often." Charlie did not sound, the judge said wryly, like a man who suffered from stupidity.

The Crown's case, the judge said, rested on both

direct and circumstantial evidence, with a great deal falling into the circumstantial category. But one piece of physical evidence — the credit-card slip, lying only feet from the garage where JoAnn met her death — had never been explained. Although Allbright and Thatcher had said the slip could have been planted there by someone who wanted to frame Colin, during the course of the trial "no explanation has . . . been given for the appearance of this credit-card slip," Justice Maher said.

The judge further instructed the jury that the taped conversation between Thatcher and Anderson was a "significant" piece of evidence and one that should be carefully considered. For that reason, there would be arrangements made for the jurors to hear the tape whenever they wanted.

The judge then turned his attention to Dotson's evidence. While Craig Dotson's description of the man who left the Wilson garage did not resemble Colin Thatcher, and the police sketch didn't resemble the politician either, Dotson had given the man only a "fleeting glance" and had said he was never satisfied with the police sketch.

By contrast with his review of the Crown's case, the judge's comments on the defence witnesses were relatively brief. He had spent a good portion of an hour on the Crown's evidence but discussed the eight witnesses who had testified on Colin's behalf for only ten minutes or so.

He labelled Tony Merchant's suggestion that the Regina police had had something to do with the disappearance of telephone records from his office "incredible": "I find it incredible that Mr. Merchant would make a suggestion that the Regina police would participate in criminal activities."

About the evidence of the other witnesses — Thatcher's sons, housekeeper, housekeeper's brother and

211

an employee's wife — the judge simply said: "It is for you to decide whether or not to accept the evidence of those witnesses." If the evidence of the witnesses raised "a reasonable doubt" about the guilt of Colin Thatcher, and if the alibi was accepted, then it was the jury's duty to acquit the man.

Allbright didn't escape the judge's charge unscathed. Justice Maher opened his address to the jurors by reviewing some of the remarks Allbright had made in his summation. Allbright had no business, he said, to bring up the cases of Donald Marshall or Susan Nelles: "To raise matters such as these is improper. You are not to be influenced by some baseless fear that you will probably make a mistake."

The jury departed and Allbright rose immediately to object to the charge. With a tense, unsmiling Thatcher looking on, Allbright called the judge's instructions one-sided. Even if Justice Maher called the jury back and recharged them, he complained, there would be no way of eliminating the implication that the "court has a preference for the theory of the Crown evidence to that of the defence evidence." The judge had concentrated on the prosecution and made almost no comment on the defence witnesses, and "the court has, with the greatest respect, pointed what I would call the judicial finger at Mr. Thatcher," the defence lawyer argued.

"You are entitled to your opinions, Mr. Allbright," Justice Maher responded coldly.

Understandably, Serge Kujawa had no objections to the judge's charge, but merely requested that if a recharge was in order perhaps the judge could place a greater emphasis on the tape.

The judge then left the courtroom. It was all over except for the waiting.

CHAPTER FOURTEEN

The Verdict

On Friday, November 2, just before noon, the seven men and five women jurors left the courtroom to consider Colin Thatcher's fate.

The first thing they did was break for lunch, making their way through the snow to the Bessborough Hotel across the street, accompanied by sheriff's officers.

Nothing is known about the jurors. The judge laid down the law early in the trial when he ruled that the names and occupations of the jurors could not be revealed. It is, of course, also standard procedure for a jury to be sequestered during its deliberations. These people stayed at the Bessborough and were not allowed phones, radios, televisions or newspapers. They were accompanied at their hotel and during their meals by members of the sheriff's department.

There had been some debate among the journalists about whether the judge's anonymity ruling also forbade the taking of photographs or television tapes as the jurors walked back and forth between hotel and courtroom. In the end, everyone filmed and photographed and used the material and there were no repercussions.

By this time, the press corps had swollen to forty or more. There were thirty-five regulars who had attended the trial every day from its beginning, plus the newcomers who filtered in to cover the verdict.

Pat Bugera, the justice department's representative, had agreed with the Canadian Press and the United Press Canada reporters to make two phone calls when the verdict came in: one call to reporters stationed at the Bessborough Hotel, and one to the media corps staying at the Ramada Renaissance.

Hospitality suites at both hotels had been set up for the media to keep their daily twelve-hour vigil. Every time the phone rang in either room over the next four days, everyone froze, ready to make the mad dash through the snow back to the courthouse.

Bugera had agreed to make the phone calls only in the event of a verdict. If the jury returned with questions or the court convened for any reason, it was up to the press to find out for themselves. A system was therefore devised, by John Ward of CP, to alert reporters to any events. The press corps was divided into sixteen two-person teams. Every hour a fresh team would loiter in the hallways of the courthouse with instructions to dash to the only pay phone in the court building if anything happened.

The deliberations officially started that afternoon at 2 p.m. At the hotels, spirits were high, as everyone predicted the jury would return within hours. Plans for the evening celebration were discussed.

At 6 p.m. the jury broke for dinner. It reconvened at 8 o'clock.

By that evening, the jurors had drafted a list of ten questions for the judge. To answer them, the judge had to recall the court reporter, have her find the appropriate sections in the testimony, and read aloud the relevant passages, both the examination and the cross-examination of each witness.

The jury wanted to know times and dates of some of the meetings between Thatcher and Anderson. They also wanted information on what colour Anderson

214

thought the gun was, and a review of the evidence of Joan Hasz and what time she saw the suspicious car outside the Wilson house.

They asked what time Anderson had turned over the .357 magnum to Colin Thatcher on the day of the murder; and they requested a review of the evidence of Anderson and Charlie Wilde relating to the meetings between Thatcher, Wilde, Crutcher and Anderson.

After hearing the questions, it was obvious to everyone in the courtroom that there would not be a verdict that night.

Arrangements were made for the jury to sleep at the Bessborough and hear the Anderson/Thatcher tape replayed first thing in the morning. The jurors retired about 10 p.m.

During most of the next morning, the court reporter reread the requested passages from the trial record, after which the jurors broke for lunch. They started their deliberations again that afternoon, and the lengthy process of reaching a verdict continued, hour after hour.

For Thatcher, it meant long hours in the holding cells on the first floor of the courthouse. His cells were clearly visible from the Ramada hotel, and occasionally he could be seen peering through the cracks in the curtains. Thatcher's family was allowed to spend time with him in the cells while the wait dragged on.

Digging for a new angle one night, a local reporter queried the man who had delivered Thatcher's dinner to the jail. True to form, Thatcher had consumed a thick T-bone steak, a salad and tomato juice.

By Saturday night, complete boredom had set in among the journalists, with many of the reporters cooling their heels in the hospitality suites. At the Ramada, most drifted down to the lounge bar where they could watch the back of the courthouse through the front doors of the hotel. The drinking started about 7 p.m.

215

— and it was probably just as well no verdict came in that night.

For the lawyers the wait was more intense. Kujawa, who never goes to bed until the early hours anyway, had perfected his own technique for jury watches. He would stretch backwards in his chair, with his feet up, and nod off to sleep within seconds. About twenty minutes later, he'd wake up, completely refreshed. Both he and Allbright maintained low profiles during the four-day vigil.

On Sunday morning, the jurors looked glum and tired. The tension appeared to be getting to them. Speculation was rife as the spectre of a hung jury loomed. The longer the jury stayed out, the better it looked for the defence, many said. Reporters tried to guess which juror might be holding the process up.

At lunchtime, the jurors appeared in the courthouse parking lot. They took a five-minute exercise break, jogging around and doing deep knee-bends, then walked back into the courthouse with their heads down.

Thatcher's mother, Peggy, and his minister, Ray Matheson from Regina, visited him that day.

For some reason that night, mounting tension drew many reporters back to the courthouse, even though they weren't scheduled to do their watch. By about 9 p.m., nearly every journalist in Saskatoon was standing quietly or sitting and reading in the hallways.

The expectant atmosphere was intensified when the two court reporters appeared in the parking lot. A short time later, the court clerk burst into the hallway and rushed into his room carrying clean court shirts. The crowd waited on edge for about ten minutes and relaxed when he reappeared in street clothes. A false alarm.

At about 9:30 p.m., the jury broke for the night and that day's vigil was over.

On Monday morning the jury asked to hear Craig Dotson's evidence again. The court reporter patiently reread it. The jury listened and left to continue their deliberations. During this time, Justice Maher sent several notes to the jury asking if they needed his assistance. They declined, saying they were making progress.

The wait was getting to everyone. Newsrooms across the country were beginning to get jumpy. Some reporters had to prepare three different sets of stories: one for a conviction, one for an acquittal and one to run in case there was a hung jury.

That evening, several journalists and Pat Bugera were waiting for an elevator at the Renaissance. They were bitching about the length of the wait and saying how it was getting on their nerves.

"Tell me about it," said a quiet voice from behind them. It was Greg Thatcher. The group immediately fell silent. If it was tough on the journalists, they could only imagine how difficult it was for the family and Thatcher himself.

Pat, who is a gracious and warm woman, immediately stepped forward and put her hand on Greg's forearm. "Never mind us," she said. "It must be very difficult for you."

She looked at him with understanding and sympathy, and added, "Of course, the longer they stay out, the better it is for you."

He agreed and followed the group onto the elevator.

The Thatcher family probably felt they never got a break. A hotel is a very closed world, and it seemed that everywhere they turned they ran into the media. They were unfailingly polite and gracious to the journalists, although considering the nature of the trial, and the coverage, they had no reason to be.

Tuesday, November 6, was like every other day of the trial — cold and snowy. In the hospitality suites, the press had just finished their breakfast and were settling in for another day of waiting. Some had already stretched out on the couches and beds, prepared to continue their morning sleep while they waited for the phone call.

They didn't have long to wait. Just after 10:30 a.m. the phone rang. It was Pat Bugera telling them to come back to the courthouse. A few seconds later, the phone rang again. This time it was Doug McConachie from the Saskatoon *Star-Phoenix*, who was doing the jury watch at the court.

Everyone ran like the wind, struggling into winter clothes and racing to collect their photographers and cameramen. A group of photographers were just digging into breakfast when the reporters burst in. The photographers jumped up, shouting at the waitress that they'd pay her later, and ran down the back alley of the courthouse.

By 10:45 a.m. everyone was in place. Surprisingly, the courtroom wasn't bursting at the seams as it had been during the testimony. The public hadn't spent hours waiting in line for the verdict as they had to see the witnesses.

The RCMP moved amazingly quickly. In the fifteen minutes between the phone call and the judge's entry into the courtroom, they managed to search everyone and scan them with metal detectors. (The search, which was carried out every morning and every afternoon from the beginning of the trial, was routine.)

The mood inside the courtroom was tense, with an overlay of excitement. Unusually, there was complete silence, with none of the shufflings and whisperings of a large expectant crowd.

Thatcher's mother, Peggy, his oldest son, Greg, and Thatcher's girlfriend, Diane Stoner, had taken their usual seats in the third row. They looked tense and tired, drained by the four-day wait.

Thatcher was brought into the courtroom. Impeccably dressed as usual, he looked at his family with no sign of emotion and took his seat in the prisoner's box at the side of the courtroom, directly in front of the jury.

Allbright, Kujawa and Johnston were in place. They sat uneasily in their chairs. Bugera came in and sat in her usual place beside the door. Deputy-Chief Swayze, Sergeant Bob Murton and retired Staff-Sergeant Wally Beaton filled the larger prisoner's box as they waited.

Two court reporters came in. The first sat in the regular spot, directly in front of the witness box. The second sat in a line of chairs at the side of the court.

Seeing both court reporters caused more speculation in the press rows. Why were two of them there? Could it be that the jury didn't have a verdict but only wanted to ask another question? That meant one reporter would read the evidence while the other one recorded it.

Thatcher continued to stare at the wall. Many of the people in the courtroom had been told to expect an outburst from him if he was convicted. The photographers and the cameramen outside the courthouse and at the jail were told by police to stay clear of Thatcher's feet. The journalists had been warned he would lash out and, since he was handcuffed, the only thing he could do was kick. No one wanted a repeat of an incident a year earlier in Toronto, at the funeral of Paul Volpe, where Joseph Volpe had flattened a CBC cameraman with a kick to the groin.

At about 10:45 a.m. the jury was brought in. More than a hundred pairs of eyes were on them as the crowd looked for a hint or a sign of what was to follow.

The foreman walked in first to take his place at the end seat of the second row of the jury box. His nickname, bestowed by the press, was Mr. G.Q. (from *Gentlemen's Quarterly*, a men's fashion magazine), because of the fashionable and well-tailored clothing he wore during the fifteen-day trial. The foreman didn't disappoint the crowd this morning. He was wearing a crisp, navy-blue, pin-striped, three-piece suit with a gold pocket watch strung across the front of his vest.

The foreman looked anxious. Twisting his hands together, possibly in an effort to keep them from shaking, he sat down and looked at the floor.

Every other jury member did the same. When all of them were seated, not one of them looked at Thatcher. They looked at the floor, the ceiling, the judge's seat, the court reporter — anywhere but at the man who was staring at them so intently from across the room.

For an instant, a flicker of panic crossed Thatcher's face as he scrutinized the twelve men and women who had knowledge of his fate. Thatcher had been so convinced during the trial of his acquittal that he had a bottle of Chivas waiting for him and two plane tickets to Palm Springs. He'd had Allbright enter him in fishing derbies and golf tournaments for the month of November. And his girlfriend, Diane, a nurse at a Regina hospital, had booked time off work because she, too, was convinced that Thatcher would walk from the courtroom that day, down the stairs and onto the street, a free man.

There was absolute silence in the minute or so that followed. The cast of characters was in place, the stage was set and the audience was ready. All they were waiting for was the director, the judge, Mr. Justice Jack Maher. But no theatre performance can match the drama of a jury bringing a verdict on a first-degree murder charge. The fate of a human being is in the balance and only twelve of the people in the room know the final outcome.

It seemed a long time until Justice Maher entered the room. Actually it was only a minute or two, but it must have been an eternity for Colin Thatcher.

"Order," the court clerk called and the audience scrambled to its feet as the judge swept into the room and up into his seat.

The clerk stood and read out the names of the jurors. They answered "present" as their names were called.

"Ladies and gentlemen of the jury have you reached a verdict?" the clerk enquired.

The foreman stood and answered in a clear, firm voice.

"Yes, we have," he said. "We find the accused guilty as charged."

Then he sat down.

Thatcher turned ashen when the verdict was spoken. He winced as if he was in pain, closed his eyes and rested his head on the wall behind the prisoner's box.

Peggy Thatcher didn't hear the verdict. She frantically and urgently spoke to her grandson.

"What did they say? What did they say?" she whispered.

Greg was looking at the ceiling, away from his father and away from the prying eyes of the media.

"Guilty," he answered his grandmother in a low voice.

She gasped and put her head down. Diane Stoner looked stunned. She sat in her seat, staring straight ahead.

Several journalists leaped from their seats and made for the door. They had immediate deadlines. Some were radio reporters whose stations wanted to issue bulletins within seconds of the verdict.

One local reporter raced out the front door of the courthouse and down the steps to find a pay phone to call her station. As she ran down the stairs, a waiting crowd of people called out to her, as a local CBC crew filmed her.

"Guilty," she cried. "Of first-degree."

Then she slipped on the ice. Her legs shot out from

under her and she bounced unceremoniously onto the wet concrete of the sidewalk. Her fall was duly recorded by the CBC cameraman, and later displayed across the country on the national news that night.

Inside the courtroom, Justice Maher wasted no time. Within seconds of the verdict he turned to Thatcher and told him to stand.

Thatcher pulled himself to his feet, simultaneously placing a small leather-bound book—a Bible?—inside the inside pocket of his suit. He stared straight ahead, right into the faces of the jury.

Thatcher surprised everyone by his calmness. He accepted the verdict almost gracefully and didn't utter a sound.

It was later reported that every person in the court-room was watching Thatcher when the verdict was called out. The report is not true. At least one person refused to look into Thatcher's face. That was Serge Kujawa. He couldn't bear to watch.

''I didn't look at Colin Thatcher,'' he said later. ''When the guy says guilty, I don't want to see the devastation on another person. I look away.''

The judge didn't waste any time with the sentencing. A veteran, he knew that the best way to end it was to do what had to be done quickly.

The sentence is automatic in a first-degree murder conviction.

Mr. Justice Maher read from the Criminal Code in a clipped, hard voice. His words fell like stones onto Colin Thatcher.

''You will be imprisoned in a federal penitentiary for life without eligibility for parole for twenty-five years,'' he said. He then told Thatcher to sit down.

Turning to the jury, the judge spoke in a softer voice.

''The court wishes to express its thanks for your diligence and attendance to the law,'' he said. He gently told them that their duty was done and they were now free to leave.

The first row of six stood and turned to their right to walk single file from the courtroom.

"I looked at all of them, and there were tears in their eyes," Kujawa said later. "I could understand that."

After the jury departed, the judge faced the body of the courtroom. "This court is now adjourned," he announced. Everyone stood as he left.

The court emptied quickly. Fifteen minutes later it stood empty, in semi-darkness, with the lights turned out. Rays of sunlight broke through the cracks of the heavy curtains and spotlighted the dust rising from the old, red, crushed-velvet seats. It was as though nothing had happened there at all that morning.

Outside was a hubbub of activity. Spectators lined the back alley, waiting to see Thatcher taken away. There were faces in every window of the office buildings surrounding the courthouse as the drama unfolded below. The press, too, milled about the back alley waiting to corner Kujawa, Allbright or the Thatcher family for reactions.

Pat Bugera escorted Kujawa and Johnston down in the elevator to a waiting crush of reporters. Kujawa spoke briefly and eloquently.

"It's not a happy moment for anybody," he said. "I'm very sad."

He called the case a "human tragedy". "It's a tragedy, especially for a man with that much obvious talent," he said.

Kujawa said he anticipated an appeal because "cases like these are always appealed. We'll see you in Ottawa." He then thanked his assistant, Al Johnston, and had special words of praise for Johnston and Ed Swayze and his staff.

Allbright had agreed to answer questions from the press, as well, but he failed to make an appearance. The scene he had with the Thatcher family and Colin in the cells was difficult for him.

"Pat, I just can't," he told Bugera when she asked

him. Bugera replied that she understood and that she hoped the press would understand as well. Allbright left the court that day, without a word, in a fast-moving van. The doors were shuttered and locked at his house and there was no one at his office.

Likewise, Thatcher's family was whisked from the courthouse in the back of a police cruiser and into the basement of the Ramada. Some photographers managed to run up alongside the cruiser for pictures while another camera crew shot pictures of the family as they got on the elevator. All of them were visibly shaken.

One reporter broke down and cried for about five minutes when his stories were filed and it was all over. It was a release from the tension. A colleague advised him not to cry, but instead to think of what had happened to JoAnn. The reporter's tears soon ceased.

One unmarked car and four police cruisers were used to escort Thatcher from the court that day. He had changed into his jeans and a hooded sweatshirt to go back to jail. The convoy pulled slowly away from the back of the courthouse while spectators waited patiently in the cold to catch their last glimpse of Colin Thatcher.

At the jail he had little to say. "I'm not going to appeal, it doesn't matter now," he said.

When asked if that meant he had given up, Thatcher replied: "I'm innocent. I did not do it, but it wasn't in the cards, and no, I will not be appealing."

He was asked if he thought he had had a fair trial. "I'm innocent, so I don't know," he replied.

He spoke in a subdued tone. There was no evidence of his usual cocksure manner or his slick tongue. He appeared quiet and resigned to his fate.

The bottle of Chivas and the Palm Springs plane tickets were going to have to wait.

Epilogue

The conviction of Colin Thatcher was received with mixed emotions by many.

Lynne Mendell felt both relief and a sense of sadness. Deputy-Chief Swayze phoned her at home about ten minutes after the verdict came in. She believes that Colin Thatcher will kill himself rather than spend the rest of his life in prison.

For Serge Kujawa, Ed Swayze, Al Johnston and Gerry Allbright, the end of the trial meant a return to normal life. All of them, after devoting months to the murder case, are back to their regular routines.

For Gary Anderson and Charlie Wilde, the end of the trial meant the start of a new life. Anderson, Wilde and Wilde's common-law wife are starting fresh, with new identities in different parts of the country.

Harlan and Betty Geiger feel that the jury's verdict was the appropriate one. They have extended their sympathy to Peggy Thatcher on an outcome that must be very difficult for her to accept. But the verdict hasn't been the end of it for the Geigers. Someone anonymously sent a cruel package to them a few weeks after the end of the trial. It contained copies of various "letters to the editor" published in the press, that have been written by people who believe Thatcher is innocent. The sender had cut all of the authors' names off.

The Thatcher children continue to live at the Redland Avenue house in Moose Jaw.

Colin Thatcher immediately launched a hunger strike in jail because he didn't like his new quarters. He was moved to a security wing. He has now appealed his conviction.

Some of his constituents in Thatcher's former riding of Thunder Creek who believe he is innocent have started a drive to raise money for a defence fund.

Tony Wilson has put the Albert Street home up for sale and is seeking oblivion in his work from the pain of his loss and the stress and upheaval of its aftermath.

The Progressive Conservative government of Saskatchewan ousted Colin Thatcher from the Legislature on November 28, 1984.

APPENDIX

Transcript of Anderson Tape Recording

ANDERSON: I'm proceeding down to Caron. Still heading down to Caron, still heading down to Caron. Just crossing the railroad tracks at Caron, just crossing the railroad tracks, just crossing the railroad tracks. Going to go in, going to go in. At entrance. He's over at the fuel tanks, I'm going over.

THATCHER: I needed gas, head up by the nuisance ground road, okay?

ANDERSON: I'll meet you up there, I'll meet you at the abandoned farm.

THATCHER: At the what?

ANDERSON: Abandoned farm.

THATCHER: Yeah, okay.

ANDERSON: Contact made, contact made, contact made. He's fuelling truck, he's fuelling truck. Going to meet at abandoned farm. I'm on my way there now. Going to meet at abandoned farm. He looked awful surprised to see me, he looked awful surprised to see me. Proceeding to Caronport, proceeding to Caronport. Proceeding to Caronport. Approaching highway, approaching highway, approaching highway. I've crossed highway, I've crossed highway, I've crossed highway. Turning north to abandoned farm, turning north to abandoned farm. Going north, going north. Going north to abandoned farm, going north to abandoned farm. Turning to go west, turning to go west to abandoned farm, turning to go west. There's a farm road on the field on my left, or on my right. A farmer in the field on my right. I don't know if that will spook him, I don't know if that will spook him. I'm going to go in anyways. I'm going to go in anyways. Turning into abandoned farm, turning into abandoned farm. I'm in the abandoned farm,

227

I'm in the abandoned farm, in the abandoned farm. My truck is beside the red Quonset, my truck is beside the red Quonset. I can pick up the sounds of that plane pretty good, I can pick up the sounds of that plane pretty good. I'm inside the barn, inside the barn. Talking quiet. Just checking the sides of the building, just checking the sides of the building. He's arriving in a little grey car, he's arriving in a little grey car.

THATCHER: Been having truck trouble, I had to — let's get in this car and go for a ride.

ANDERSON: I'd prefer to stay around, I just — I only wanted to be a couple of minutes.

THATCHER: All right.

ANDERSON: Just so we can . . . . So, I haven't seen you around, how you been keeping?

THATCHER: Fine. I thought I saw you from a distance.

ANDERSON: Yeah, well . . .

THATCHER: Have to be awfully cautious, one never knows. . . . Is everything okay with you?

ANDERSON: Yeah, not bad, I guess.

THATCHER: How long are you around for?

ANDERSON: Friday. How does the — you guys getting ready to start seeding?

THATCHER: Well, I've been away, I just got back last night.

ANDERSON: Uh-huh.

THATCHER: I haven't seen and I couldn't get the truck started this morning, and when you pulled out of the yard, but . . .

ANDERSON: Land's dry.

THATCHER: Yeah, it is. It's really down at this end, this is where Evan Thally used to dump his manure. Well, everything is — let's walk over this way. Everything is — there's no problem, have you been hassled?

ANDERSON: Well, they came once and talked to me and just asked me about the Chev car, and that was about it. Other than that, nothing at all. How about you?

THATCHER: Just the once, the day after, and that was — they — no question, there's been some attempts to put us together and we should not be seen together.

ANDERSON: Okay.

THATCHER: They've pulled some—I'll tell you, they've pulled some cheap stunts. Well, for instance, pulled a stunt like the—Wayne's sister-in-law, once last summer they came to there, they went to the door of his barn, there, and asked for you. You know, just to see what her reaction. Of course, and that never—

ANDERSON: Yeah.

THATCHER: —never heard of you.

ANDERSON: Yeah.

THATCHER: You know, you hear all sorts of wild rumours, but . . .

ANDERSON: Well, I've been out of circulation.

THATCHER: Where you been?

ANDERSON: Up north.

THATCHER: What—were you—did you have a government job?

ANDERSON: Yup.

THATCHER: Who with?

ANDERSON: DNS.

THATCHER: DNS. Well they spent some time trying to connect me, getting you up—getting you that job.

ANDERSON: Hmm.

THATCHER: Are you working for them now?

ANDERSON: No, I'm on holidays.

THATCHER: Right.

ANDERSON: I took some time off.

THATCHER: But I mean, you've still got a job with them, have you?

ANDERSON: Yeah, but—everything's—it's on a contract, eh, you know?

THATCHER: Uh-huh.

ANDERSON: Terminated a day's notice, two day's notice. Whatever they hell—whatever the hell they feel like, so. Everything went okay though, eh?

THATCHER: Yeah, there's no connection back. I saw Jane Graham, in California about a week ago, and they were up—well it sounded like they were trying to hang something onto him, because Beaton, who's handled the investigation, was in Calgary, seeing him on April the 11th.

ANDERSON: Mhmm.

THATCHER: Jane wasn't supposed to know about it. Well, you know, they're up to that. I can't figure it out, I don't know.

ANDERSON: I got rid of the stuff out of the car.

THATCHER: Good.

ANDERSON: You kind of give me a scare there with — I found the stuff lying in there and then I wondered what the hell — I didn't know where the hell you — what the hell you'd done with the gun?

THATCHER: Don't even talk like that, don't — don't even — walk out this way a little, away from the car. Now, there are no loose ends, at all, and, you know, they've gone — every which direction. Was there any way a loose end from a couple of years ago can ever resurface, from some of the guys that — discussing some business with, is there any way there's ever been a problem surface from them?

ANDERSON: You mean from Vancouver and Winnipeg? I located one of them.

THATCHER: The one that I met, or the other one?

ANDERSON: The other one.

THATCHER: Son of a bitch.

ANDERSON: Well, it's up to you.

THATCHER: Is he in — he's not in jail now, is he, or in any trouble?

ANDERSON: Not to my knowledge.

THATCHER: Is he about to cause any problems?

ANDERSON: I don't know. He didn't exactly recognize me.

THATCHER: Oh, okay.

ANDERSON: Like, I know who he is, but I don't think he has — knows who I am or has connected me.

THATCHER: Okay, I'll — I'm going to tell you something my lawyer told me, and he had heard this on a real rumour basis. There's just a rumour, and of course, there's been fifty thousand rumours. I heard this, oh, almost a year ago, and this is from Merchant.

ANDERSON: Mhmm.

THATCHER: Some guy in Alberta, by the name of Eddie Johnson, on a plea bargain, said. ''I got the answer to the Thatcher thing.''

ANDERSON: Mhmm.

THATCHER: And as the story — and he told this bizarre story of a meeting in the LaSalle Hotel, with Harry Kangles, and me, Tony Merchant.

ANDERSON: Mhmm.

THATCHER: Somebody else, and the killer. The killer was never identified. They apparently took it very seriously and they even pulled Kangles in and —

ANDERSON: Mhmm.

THATCHER: — gave a lie detector. I mean, everybody laughed at the story, including me, but does any of that have any familiarity to you at all?

ANDERSON: Nothing at all.

THATCHER: I think there's been some crap, like, what gets them going. I think somebody gets made for something —

ANDERSON: Mhmm.

THATCHER: And then I think, you know, as they say, "I know what happened," and he'll make up sort of a fabrication and they'll, you know, start running around. Do you need some bread?

ANDERSON: Yeah, I can use some. I can use some for that car.

THATCHER: Okay.

ANDERSON: How about Friday, in the afternoon?

THATCHER: Yeah.

ANDERSON: Pick a time, later in the afternoon the better.

THATCHER: Okay, I'll. . . . Okay, now there's — we got wild oats coming. We got no problem. There is no problem. You and I have any distance — keep a distance. We've got to be very careful around Caronport because Royden is the mouth there.

ANDERSON: Mhmm.

THATCHER: I know they've been to see him.

ANDERSON: Mhmm.

THATCHER: A multitude of times and I know they'd love to just catch you and I conversing. So, I'll tell you what I'll do, I'll round some up, I'm really strapped right now, but I'll round some up. And what I'd prefer to do is leave it somewhere, and I don't think we should even converse again for a good number of months.

ANDERSON: Okay. Any idea where? Do you want to leave it here?

231

THATCHER: I can leave it —

ANDERSON: Hey, hey, why don't you just leave it, why don't you take it and throw it in a plastic bag, in an envelope, and throw it in the coulee back there?

THATCHER: Well —

ANDERSON: Hey, I don't have to get out of the vehicle and drive in, just — I don't want to be seen here with my vehicle. This is last trip I want to come in with it. I just — you know as well as I do it — like you said, we don't want to be seen. What was I going to ask you? — okay . . .

THATCHER: I always have a great fear of those parabolic mikes that they have.

ANDERSON: Yeah. Well, I'd prefer it in the open. Okay, is there — okay — let me see — okay — yeah. Okay, is there anything else that you want to. . . ?

THATCHER: No, just — remember that car, that orange car that you used to have, has it disappeared?

ANDERSON: Which one? Orange one?

THATCHER: Yeah.

ANDERSON: You mean the brown one.

THATCHER: The brown one, yeah. Whichever—the stuff that was left, you know.

ANDERSON: You mean the jacket and that? I got rid of that.

THATCHER: The car, too?

ANDERSON: The car was cleaned and sold.

THATCHER: Okay.

ANDERSON: That really screwed me because I'd—like at that time I needed that money.

THATCHER: Yeah. Okay, you — he's just driving slow there.

ANDERSON: Let's walk.

THATCHER: What?

ANDERSON: Let's walk over to here. Let's get in behind the barn.

THATCHER: You go back there, I'll walk over here.

ANDERSON: Okay.

THATCHER: There is no question my phones are bugged. They probably always will be. I'm just wondering — tell you what, how about I just leave a garbage bag stuck right there?

ANDERSON: Okay.

THATCHER: Okay. And — did they hassle you at all?

ANDERSON: Just to the point of they asked about the Chevy. That was about it.

THATCHER: Yeah.

ANDERSON: You know they haven't — you say hassle, I'm assuming you know, haul you into a room and beat you with a rubber hose, or something, no.

THATCHER: Well, remember you don't — remember your rights, you don't even have to talk to them

ANDERSON: Yeah, but what do I do for a lawyer if I'm strapped, who do I get? I'm — this should never come, I mean, you can't very well go for a legal aid lawyer.

THATCHER: Why?

ANDERSON: There isn't any good ones.

THATCHER: Oh well, don't worry about that, but I mean, it ain't coming to that. It ain't coming to that 'cause they have no way of — there's only two places to put the connection together, and they got zero else. They've got zero else, and I mean you know what there is to put together and it ain't possible, and it ain't coming from me. I mean, just always remember that if you were ever to say that I said this or that, it's a crock of garbage. It's just always deny, deny, deny.

ANDERSON: Mhmm.

THATCHER: Because no matter what it was, you know. And, you know, I was just lucky that night, I was home with four people. Four people, pretty solid, and that's pretty hard. What about you, are you covered at the time?

ANDERSON: Yup.

THATCHER: Well, then there's, you know, that's — I didn't know about you, but —

ANDERSON: Yeah, but under questioning or if something ever happens, would they ever crack those — your witnesses?

THATCHER: No. Never.

ANDERSON: Never?

THATCHER: Never.

ANDERSON: No?

THATCHER: Never, never, never. They tried. They worked on Sandra, they showed her a variety of photographs. They showed her one of you, and one of Larry, and anybody that had a beard about that time, they showed photographs. They were showing photographs of a young

233

guy. I never saw him, but they were flashing them around Caronport. I never—they never showed them to me. They, you know, their trick is, their style was they—somebody that they're talking to, their style is, ''Well, listen, we know that he did it, and we're close to it, and we know that you know.'' Something like this. And then they'll start showing these pictures. When, in fact, they don't. They—you know, I mean, they're just fishing.

ANDERSON: Mhmm.

THATCHER: And, like—oh, they tried to—they tried to crack Sandra, and there was just . . .

ANDERSON: Oh, I had a hell of a time to clean the car out.

THATCHER: Is that right?

ANDERSON: Yeah. I had a bitch of a time getting the blood and stuff off.

THATCHER: Yeah. Is there no chance that it can ever surface. There is a chance it can surface?

ANDERSON: No, I don't—no.

THATCHER: Okay.

ANDERSON: The car was cleaned.

THATCHER: Okay.

ANDERSON: I didn't burn it, but it was cleaned.

THATCHER: All right. They—as I say, the only—the only link that they've got—when you want to see me just—like this again—just give me that—I'd have gone right up there, I was out of gas.

ANDERSON: Okay, the next — if we should ever, ever, ever have to meet again, okay?

THATCHER: Well, we will.

ANDERSON: Okay, we'll meet at that other abandoned place.

THATCHER: Okay.

ANDERSON: Okay, by Hous's.

THATCHER: Okay.

ANDERSON: And then you can — well it's just away from here, because I don't want to be back in here again.

THATCHER: Okay, okay. Are we — is that the only — that is the only connection and the only other one is those ones that we're talking business with over two — almost two years ago. Unless one of those — the other guy, the one was here, is he still in — is he still in Manitoba?

234

ANDERSON: I'm assuming. I'm close to coming onto that, but I haven't had the opportunity to really get into it. I just happened to run into the other one by very, very — quite by accident. I was asking some people and just sort of checking around and I found him. He doesn't know me.

THATCHER: You know, should go just visit that son of a bitch some day, but not right now, not right now. Now, there is no problem. There are no other loose ends, eh? I mean, you know what the ends were and obviously I ain't a loose end and you're not, and there's nothing—there's nothing to come to. I mean, I think they've done a lot of speculating and a lot of guessing, but, you know, if — they originally got eighteen guys on it and they're down to—well, I don't know whether anybody's on it all the time, but I do know that Beaton was up in — talking to Graham two weeks ago — well that's, you know. That tells you —

ANDERSON: Mhmm.

THATCHER: — something. I mean.

ANDERSON: What's Beaton like?

THATCHER: Oh, he's a nice guy, but they're all—I don't trust any of them, they're, you know, I think what happens is I think the thing just sits dormant and then I think some guy that's an umpteen-time loser tries to make a plea bargain or something, and makes up a cock and —

ANDERSON: Mhmm.

THATCHER: — bull story that he knows something and of course it goes on the channels and they start running around again. That's sort of my guess. Because they — incidentally, Friday afternoon, I won't — I'll put the stuff here, sometime on Friday. You're leaving on Friday, are you?

ANDERSON: Mhmm.

THATCHER: All right, I'll put the stuff there sometime on Friday and I'll put as much as I can get there without suspicion. Slip back, you know, a little bit, you know, in a couple of months if you have to. There—as long as there's nobody—we just don't want to be seen, but the next time, meet you on the road.

ANDERSON: Mhmm.

THATCHER: If you go like that with your hand.

ANDERSON: Mhmm, mhmm.

THATCHER: I know what you mean, five minutes up in that spot, and —

ANDERSON: Okay.

THATCHER: If I'm, you know, unless I'm with somebody or something, if I'm not there within five minutes, I mean, it will be as fast as I can get rid of who's ever with me. Okay?

ANDERSON: Okay.

THATCHER: If I'm by myself, I'll go right there. But, you know, there's no problem unless something stupid's done, now, and I'll pull what I safely can, and, but I just don't want to do something stupid in this stage of the game. But, next time, slip back, give me that — don't drive in my yard again, though. There's no problem, I know, I know, I saw you and I couldn't come because I thought I was going to run out of gas any minute.

ANDERSON: Oh.

THATCHER: And, I would have.

ANDERSON: That's — I didn't stick around. I just — in and out.

THATCHER: Okay, and just remember there are no — there's no problems and there won't be unless they trip over something and I got no intention of giving them anything to trip on. There are no loose ends like, you know, there's nothing for them to find, you know.

ANDERSON: It's all been taken care of.

THATCHER: All, sure. Heavens, yes, heavens, yes. I still don't trust the bastards for bugs. I mean, I don't know whether there's any possibility that that — that's why when we talk, just assume the bastards are listening.

ANDERSON: Okay.

THATCHER: Don't give them any information. You taught me that. Remember, they got that one guy three years later.

ANDERSON: Mhmm.

THATCHER: And certainly never call, okay, on the telephone. But no question, no question, I'm bugged.

ANDERSON: No. What am I going to do if you change parties?

THATCHER: I'm not changing parties. I ain't changing parties.

ANDERSON: You like where you sit, eh?

THATCHER: Well, I'll tell you, they're getting into a little bit of trouble now, with Sveinson, and then those two guys

236

this morning that went to the Liberals. All of a sudden Devine likes to talk to an old pro again there.

ANDERSON: Does he?

THATCHER: Yes, all of a sudden, yeah, it's — yeah, he called me in California and —

ANDERSON: Maybe he wants your seat?

THATCHER: No, no, no. I don't think that, no. You know, he can't have that. And — no, things are slipping away from him and I think he's starting to know it, so —

ANDERSON: Mhmm.

THATCHER: I'm falling back into favour again, even though I really don't care one way or the other. Sort of like it where I'm sitting right now. Okay I'll . . .

ANDERSON: Well, like . . .

THATCHER: Like I say, there ain't . . . I've been curious to know whether or not they hassled you or not, because, no question, your name came up when they talked to Greg. And, you know, they just slipped it in and Greg, oh yeah, sure. They've been through me with a fine-tooth comb.

ANDERSON: Could I — if I had to get a lawyer, could I get Merchant?

THATCHER: Oh, I think so.

ANDERSON: Is he familiar on . . .

THATCHER: Nope.

ANDERSON: No?

THATCHER: Zero. Knows zero. But it ain't coming to that.

ANDERSON: Well . . .

THATCHER: Do you have some feeling it is?

ANDERSON: Not really, but it's like everything else. We went second — well, basically went one step further, you know, really.

THATCHER: Well, it ain't coming to that because, you know, you're covered that night. No question. Like they're not . . . As long as you're covered that night there's not a hell of a lot they can do. Are you covered good?

ANDERSON: Mhmm.

THATCHER: Well, then . . .

ANDERSON: I was . . . Well, I'm covered.

THATCHER: Don't even tell me. But if you're covered good that night, there isn't anything. And they got no interest in you anyway. It's me.

ANDERSON: Mhmm.

THATCHER: Just only as a . . . you know, and then one of the great rights that you get in this country is they have to give you . . . and you don't have to take a legal aid lawyer. But, for instance, if you haven't got the cash for it, they're, you know, you get the chance to get a hell of a lawyer and the court pays for it. That's one of the things that . . . I mean, that's the least of your problems.

ANDERSON: Yeah.

THATCHER: You can almost name who it is. Oh, yeah, that is the least of your problems. But just remember, it's, you know, deny, deny, deny. Sure, you know me as a constituent. Sure, you've rented some land. Now they've never asked about me, but, you know, sure. I've rented some land from him and, yeah, sure, they did ask my office about, like, that you had a government job. They pedalled to Royden and he said, "Well, you know, we know he got him a government job." I didn't get you any DNS one. Of course, I'd given your name to SMDC.

ANDERSON: Mhmm.

THATCHER: But, you know, they were just pulling through everything. But, you know, if they ever come up to you, sure, you know, just tell them the general stuff.

ANDERSON: Mhmm.

THATCHER: Sure, had coffee with him in Caronport. Now I haven't seen him for a year and a half or two years.

ANDERSON: Mhmm.

THATCHER: Well, there's. . . . If nothing's happening with you, you would have the feeling, because nothing is happening with me. Like I say, I think they get in . . . I think some guy that's bucked to go up the river makes a cock and bull story up to get them running again . . .

ANDERSON: Mhmm.

THATCHER: . . . running around. But if they ain't hassling you then there's nothing going on. I didn't know how heavy they'd leaned on you.

ANDERSON: What. . . . Okay. Well, I'm glad it went down.

THATCHER: Yeah. If they ain't leaned on you, then they, well, then they're . . .

ANDERSON: I'm glad it's over.

THATCHER: Yeah.

ANDERSON: You know.

THATCHER: So am I. Well, if they like, if they haven't been leaning on you and they were in Alberta two weeks ago, I mean, what's that tell you?

ANDERSON: They're still fishing.

THATCHER: Sure they are. Totally. Totally. Totally. In fact, it sounds, Janie thought they were looking hard at her husband. Couldn't care less.

ANDERSON: Still got visions of him?

THATCHER: Not particularly.

ANDERSON: How's your feelings with your old buddy Gerry . . .

THATCHER: (Laughter)

ANDERSON: . . . Gerry Gerrand.

THATCHER: Well . . .

ANDERSON: Kind of mellow to him.

THATCHER: No. A guy I could do. That guy I could do. Yeah, it's . . . oh, I'll tell you, they've tried every goddamn gimmick in the world on me. They have tried set-ups, like a guy from Ontario had to see me at the Leg.

ANDERSON: Mhmm.

THATCHER: You know, it's the story about: "I'm in the same situation you are: can you give me a name, can you give a phone number?"

ANDERSON: (Laughter)

THATCHER: Didn't know whether to laugh or cry. So I played out the role and I said, "I don't know what they're talking about." And I said, "Even if I did know what you're talking about, which I haven't the slightest idea, obviously I couldn't, and I don't believe you're who you say you are." He said, "Well check me out." I said, "No, I ain't going to check you out."

ANDERSON: Mhmm.

THATCHER: Anyway, it was the crudest set-up. But, you know, they tried garbage like this. And they'll, you know, like when they come in and they started leading up to, "We know this and we know that and we know this." When they really don't, they're fishing.

ANDERSON: Well, I hadn't heard a hell of a lot, just what you read and see in the papers.

THATCHER: Well, I didn't know how things have changed.

ANDERSON: That fucking car story went from so many fucking different extremes I didn't know if they were coming or going. And they didn't know if it was green, black, purple, orange, pink.

THATCHER: Well they sure went on a shopping mission for green Cordobas that night in Regina. But for about a month afterwards there, if you owned a green Cordoba they would knock on your door. It was. . . . Yeah, it was really bizarre.

ANDERSON: I think . . .

THATCHER: However, let's not push it. I think we should move on.

ANDERSON: Okay.

THATCHER: Well, I'll tell you what, I'll put her in a garbage bag and I'll dump her here. Next time I see you, just give me that same sign and there is no problem unless you do something stupid.

ANDERSON: Okay.

THATCHER: Okay?

ANDERSON: Yeah. I'm glad you got her.

THATCHER: Okay.

ANDERSON: See you.

THATCHER: You bet.